TYPOLOGY THEN AND NOW

Hippocrates	Adler	Horney	Dreikurs	Levin	Sheldon	Kfir	Borgata
sanguine	useful	towards	attention	democratic	affection	pleasing	responsible
choleric	ruling	against	power	autocratic	assertive	superiority	assertive
melancholy	avoiding	away	disable	lass. faire	privacy	comfort	emotion
phlegmatic	getting		revenge			control	intelligence

Raymond Corsini. Journal of Individual Psychology, Nov. 1974

Other publications by Nira Kfir

Crisis Intervention Verbatim. Hemisphere Publishing, Washington, 1989.

Challenging Cancer: From Chaos to Control, with Dr Maurice Slevin. 2nd edition, Class Publishing Ltd., London, 2002.

Understanding Suicide Terror Through Humanistic and Existential Psychology, in: Stout, Chris E., (Ed.) *The Psychology of Terrorism*. Vol.1. Praeger Publishing, Westport, CT. 2002.

PERSONALITY & PRIORITIES

A Typology

Nira Kfir

Translated from the Hebrew by
Mertyn Malkinson

Editorial Assistance by
Janet Terner

authorHOUSE®

AuthorHouse™
1663 Liberty Drive
Bloomington, IN 47403
www.authorhouse.com
Phone: 1-800-839-8640

Maagalim Publishing, Tel Aviv, Israel
maagalim@netvision.net.il

© 2011 Nira Kfir. All rights reserved.

No part of this book may be reproduced, stored in a retrieval system, or transmitted by any means without the written permission of the author.

First published by AuthorHouse 8/24/2011

ISBN: 978-1-4567-9536-8 (sc)
ISBN: 978-1-4567-9535-1 (hc)
ISBN: 978-1-4567-9537-5 (e)

Library of Congress Control Number: 2011915364

Printed in the United States of America

Any people depicted in stock imagery provided by Thinkstock are models, and such images are being used for illustrative purposes only.
Certain stock imagery © Thinkstock.

Because of the dynamic nature of the Internet, any web addresses or links contained in this book may have changed since publication and may no longer be valid. The views expressed in this work are solely those of the author and do not necessarily reflect the views of the publisher, and the publisher hereby disclaims any responsibility for them.

To Ray Corsini – teacher and friend,
who enthusiastically opened a door for me

ACKNOWLEDGEMENTS

Personality Priorities (PP) would have remained just an idea if it had not been for a great many friends who enthusiastically adopted it.

Janet Terner who organized PP workshops in Washington for several years; Dr. Lillian Beatty, President of the Social Psychiatry Association in London, who gave PP a respected place on stage;

Fifi Vervelidis, who organized seminars on PP in Athens; and

Dr. Maurice Slevin, oncologist, co-author of our book *Challenging Cancer: From Chaos to Control*, who introduced PP and translated it for his work with cancer patients.

I also want to acknowledge my good friends on the staff of "Ma'agalim" who encouraged writing this book and stubbornly insisted that PP should not remain an oral tradition. Chief among them is Tilly Milner, who has assisted me over the years, in styling and translating all the English texts, and Ruti Kamer who was in charge of typing and correcting this work and made sure it got published.

Friends on the staff who added clarifications and applications, listened and corrected include Moshe Hamiel, Dr. Michal Mor, Dr.Yael Baharav, and Efrat Kfir-Yehene.

Thank you partners, Nira Kfir
Tel Aviv
July 2011.

CONTENTS

Introduction	1
Early Learning	5
The Impasse	13
Impasse — Psychological Aspects	19
The Superior	35
The Pleaser	45
The Controller	55
The Avoider	63
Social Ecology: The Four Types	71
Case Study - Dani and Yaffa	73
Conclusion	93
Tables	96
References	101

INTRODUCTION

How Was Typology Created?

The need for man to recognize one another is imprinted within. We are intelligent creatures who observe and discriminate. The need to classify situations and people is first of all existential and practical, and is related to the flow of consciousness by the brain and the urge to interpret, understand, and respond or take action. Basically it is a need to think through, or to settle an issue. Despite the accumulated knowledge in human anthropology, this area is still physically and conceptually un-deciphered, and the process of unraveling is still an intellectual and social challenge. Psychologists have made it a lifetime study, and in addition to the well known theories, each of them evolves his own personal theory for understanding mankind.

The earliest description of types can be traced back to the ancient Greeks who classified men into pigmy, astheni and athletic types; each endowed with a physical constitution, a personal temperament and a capacity for different characteristic mental sicknesses. In effect this has remained the basic template with minor variations through the centuries and cultures. Even the Jewish Passover *Haggadah* depicts four types of sons, but in contrast to psychological typology it does not hesitate to define them as good, bad or naïve. Modern psychology is very reluctant to make value judgments; it emphasizes the differences and the legitimization of each type. Psychology, *de natura*, concerns itself with explanations of the development of types, processes, imprinting, etc.

I have often been asked what made me take up the typological approach for diagnosis and treatment, and I have been hard put to reply. However, the question brings back a flood of childhood memories. I grew up in Jerusalem and in the kindergarten - first grade years, my mother, my sister and I would eat lunch together at the "menza," the students' restaurant located at the university. We all got there at different times and I (aged 5 and a half) arrived first but had to wait for two hours for my mother and sister. I, however, was lucky because at the cash register sat a nice student called Dani who sold luncheon vouchers. He adopted me and let me sit alongside him on a low stool by the electric fire where I did my homework.

Dani was a born teacher and tried to teach me the rudiments of life. He instructed me to watch the sales counter. From where I sat, I could see only the customers' hands giving him the money for the meal tickets. Dani said: "Look at the customers' hands, and tell me what differences you see among them. Did you notice that some of them can't part with their money — putting their coins down slowly, after rummaging through their pockets or purse to put the necessary sum together? Others seem to have no problem parting with money — flinging the coins on the counter, without counting it out or stopping an ongoing conversation with a friend, — as if money has no interests for them." And so Dani would distract me from my lessons and quiz me whether I had learned to identify the person whose fingers I had seen, counting or tossing the coins. It was much later that I felt that these precious hours spent at the "menza" were such a significant experience.

In the first years of my practice in psychotherapy, I would observe my clients in order to form my first impressions. Every morning when I looked at my appointments diary, I experienced a difference in my expectations of meetings with them. Some of the names filled me with boundless energy, while others left me with a feeling of tardiness and a lack of anticipation. My instinctive reactions sparked my curiosity. When I brought them up at supervision sessions with colleagues, I discovered that we all had similar feelings. In those early days we were occupied with the chicken-egg paradox; whether the feelings of anticipating a meeting with the client were affecting us more than they did the client? Was there some kind of heterogeneity of which we were unaware regarding interactions with others?

The stimulus to organize the harvest of observations occurred while I was completing my doctoral studies at the Sorbonne in Paris. Nothing had prepared me for the culture shock that awaited me on my return to Tel Aviv at the end of the sixties. In the process of recovering from the shock I began to make comparisons: "This is what we do, and this is what they do," a comparison and differentiation based on generalizations of "them" and "us."

These years led me to gradually create in my mind an outline of typology. I reviewed the universality of the theory together with my French colleagues and clients. I consider that a theory, especially a typology, should not be restricted to one land or culture; its application should be universal. It has taken me many years of work in diverse countries before I could adopt Personality Priorities (PP) as a general typological system.

PP is subdivided into types, in particular *vis-a-vis* the interrelation of the person and his/her place within its cultural context, it is a viable strategy for identifying the principle by which each of us builds and preserves our place and the feeling of a significant existence within the human experience. During the formative years of the PP idea, I first read the book by my friend and mentor, Viktor Frankl (1946), *Man's Search for Meaning*, and on which I shall amplify later. At this point I can say that finding a place of belonging in this world is essentially a search for significance, in that significance is derived from our fellow man. In doing so, PP is the way that each of us takes to find significance through our special individuality.

Rabbi Yehuda HaNasi asks in *Pirkei Avot* (Ethics of the Fathers): "*What route should a man choose for himself?*" With all modesty I shall attempt to offer several alternatives, some of them readily observed and others that I came to define during the course of my working life. Moreover we should remember that man is much more than the sum of his IQ index, his PP type, etc. I am using PP here as social behavioral strategies that are certainly dependent on each person's variability and creativity. Two people characterized by the same priority will probably differ in their other traits.

I shall try to avoid the "Procrustean bed" of human classification because PP is designed primarily for treatment and consultation, for widening and not restricting objectives.

EARLY LEARNING

Since the rule of priorities deals with imprinting in early life, this course will begin with an introduction to early learning theories, especially those developed in the twentieth century. In early life, learning is direct, free of normative adaptation, and imprinted immediately in the brain. Our reactions to various vital events are formed and determined in these early years.

Learning can be defined as the process whereby new information becomes assimilated with pre-existing knowledge and becomes an ongoing long term feature.

I have constructed the theory of Priorities on the assumption that in early life we have certain experiences that become imprinted or fixed in our brains. These originate from negative first learnings, that create a construct over time or Impasse. An impasse, signals a blocked route ahead of us. An absolute avoidance strategy is formed from society-dependent situations in which there are memories of negative, harmful and paralyzing experiences.

In the twentieth century, many scientists devoted themselves to understanding the learning process. Besides the research, disputes and the thick tomes that were published, only a few researchers such as

Pavlov and Skinner succeeded in becoming renowned. The question how we learn intrigued behavioral researchers, brain scientists, physicists, philosophers and many others. The theoreticians of learning, headed by Watson and Thorndike, Hale and Lindsay among others, whose works were published in the first half of the twentieth century, hypothesized that in the early stage of the infant's development, the first imprinted behavioral learning is actually negative. As is typical of theoreticians, violent arguments broke out over these basic questions. Watson and Thorndike, who were active during the first three decades of the twentieth century, were divided on the issue of the relationship between learning, reward and punishment. Many years of animal experimentation left the field open for speculation, which in part was clarified only at the end of the 20th century by brain researchers. In 1950 Hilgard summed it up by saying; "there are no rules of learning that can be taught with confidence."

What is negative learning? All spontaneous behavior of an infant that is rewarded with a consistent negative response constitutes learning, an infant's brain learns to link and connect its behavior to punishment. A negative response can be a face screwing up with anger, raising the voice, raising a threatening hand, aggression in the form of taking a toy from the infant, slamming a door, allowing continuous crying with no response, and thousands more parental responses that are or aren't intended to educate or teach, or are just an angry response on the part of the parent. There are also responses that the infant, like adults throughout history, link to his behavior, even if there is no link whatever. The threat itself is interpreted as a cause of events even if there is no connection between them. A similar situation is the offering of sacrifices in a war waged on drought, or many social and religious rituals linking natural phenomena and man's behavior.

The logic behind the thesis that negative experiences actually constitute the first strong imprint is that they are consistent. Positive behavior of the baby, like drinking all the milk in the bottle receives a positive response for only a short time: "Lovely; Good boy!" As time passes the parents assume that the child's adaptation to what is required of him is expected and there's no need to praise him for it, whereas negative behavior like making a noise, aggression, clumsiness, or breaking objects invariably gets a negative reaction. When we say that "learning" has occurred, we are expected to explain in greater detail how first learning takes place. We are still talking about "personality," which is only beginning to be formed — in the brain's mechanical machine. The human brain has two main functions: Reception and processing of data, and producing energy for reaction and action.

I will briefly discuss recent explanations of how the infant's brain recognizes the outside world, and translates the information into energy-directed behavior.

Right Brain — Left Brain

How do people communicate with each other? How does one brain read the signs emanating from the other? How does the brain translate words, signs, voice, and facial expressions? Where does the brain carry out the information processing? The left hemisphere of the brain presents an analytic construct rather than an intuitive one, or a concept of detail rather than one of completeness. While the right hemisphere processes from the whole to its parts this is constructive and original thinking that is not necessarily dependent on logic. This is the division and the link between the two brains that are imprinted within us, and in all mammals, throughout evolution. Information processing is interpreted differently by the two brains, and our impression of a particular person is made up by processing a host of items visible and invisible to the eye.

In creating a link between people, and particularly when we are discussing a significant link, we "feel felt" — that we have been acknowledged and understood — by the person. In other words, our brain receives information and processes it to sensitize or personalize us *vis-à-vis* the data that was received. All this processing is actually constituted and takes place in different neurons in our brain. Avoiding contact is linked for the most part to this activity, and abstract ideas such as freedom or justice are the product of a physiological event which is highly convoluted.

Complex systems like the human brain rely on all their parts functioning, even the minutest. When a signal is received differently, it is able to affect the outcome of the thought process or even the general mind-set. In chaos theory, this is known as the "butterfly effect." The butterfly example posits that if a small butterfly flutters its wings somewhere in the world, at the other end of the earth a typhoon could develop. We can't state that the butterfly caused the typhoon; rather it initiated a chain of events beyond its power and range of intentions. A small change in one of the synapses that translate information could change completely our overall impression. Another example would be the collection of intelligence data: the addition of a single fact can change the way the analyst interprets the overall situation.

Those nerve tracts that can read signs and translate them, are also operational in the relations we form with others. For some people relationship and closeness create much satisfaction and even happiness, while others interpret closeness as "nullifying the ego" and avoid it. The various interpretations stem from translation of the inter-personal experiences, beginning at birth according to the signs and signals that produce in us a negative or positive response.

- The development of personality is a process initiated by basic feelings such as pleasure or discomfort, and progresses to the creation of sophisticated categories of emotions identified as fear, anger, disgust, surprise, interest, shame and happiness. Such feelings are complex, and require systematic sophistication in their formation. Nevertheless we should remember that they always begin as basic cerebral responses of good and bad, pleasant and unpleasant.

Does the brain block the mutual effects of processing information and taking a stand, for even an instant? Are we continuously occupied with "thinking about thought?" Daniel Siegel (1999), in his book *The Developing Mind*, called this development and streaming in our brains, "super-awareness." Super-awareness is constructed by a broadening activity of thousands of signs and signals that act together to form a mind-set. This streaming does not stop for a moment. Our mind-set is the product of two of the central roles of the brain, information and energy — information becomes energy that in turn becomes a mind-set or feeling or behavior. Each and every mind set or emotion involves thousands of cerebral activities. One can say that the "ego" is not subdivided arbitrarily between the conscious and subconscious, rather it is formed by subconscious processes of which we are unaware, and only a small portion of them penetrate our consciousness and become recognized. Simply stated, man is more complex than just his awareness element.

Our consciousness or cognition lets us connect and control, plan and understand, and experience self-consciousness. Consciousness allows us to choose in contrast to most of the complex interconnections in our brain which don't permit a conscious choice.

This concept presented by two outstanding workers in the field — Marian Solomon and Daniel Siegel, is a modern idea, as opposed to the linear model of Pavlov, Thorndike, Watson and Skinner. The modern conception doesn't see a clear link between stimulus and response, but instead, draws upon the connections of thousands of links, each of them interconnected. This resembles quantum physics which is based on Newton's laws of gravity, and determines that **A** doesn't cause **B**, rather that all the eventualities, big and small, are items of significance and their composition forms a new situation. When adapted to our field, effects are not formed directly by major force acting on a lesser one, rather they resemble more a "butterfly effect," where each unit, even the smallest, can have an effect.

A brief review of 20th century psychology demonstrates that there is much similarity to the development of physics in that century, with one exception; psychology has created personality theories that are supported by premises, observations, and the genius of a few. By that I mean today's personality theories can be traced back to the seminal genius derived from Freud's causality-based, determined approach and Adler's undetermined, purpose-driven approach for basic insight and understanding of man's motivation and behavior.

In this respect, both Freud and Adler and many others who followed, identified one core factor as the central principle of personality. The same factor was presented by psychologists as external to man himself. Freud viewed the parents, especially the mother, as a basic component in organizing the personality. Frankel in following Adler viewed the search for significance as a universal drive. Maslow presented the basic needs in the form of a pyramid that evolves into a hierarchy of advanced needs. Moreover in constructing the theory of Personality Priorities we should use modern thinking for a comparison. This thinking is affected by two principle sources: modern physics and recent research on brain development. I will present here in brief the tenets that strongly affect modern physics, the transition from the Newtonian concept to quantum physics. The Newtonian viewpoint dominated thinking in the 17th and 18th centuries, only to be called the classical science that claimed that every event is predetermined by pre-existing conditions. In this world, chance has no role, every incoming part must fall into place according to a logical sequence.

Laplace, a leading scientist, expanded on his well known hypothesis. If all the details of a certain state of the system are known — one could predict and retrodict all other states of the system. His original expression was 'to retrodict the past,' in other words, everything depends on collating facts and understanding their inter-connection.

The same mechanistic view of the universe as a simple structure that is accountable, affected not only scientific development but spread to parallel disciplines. In our opinion the founders of modern psychology who in turn were influenced, especially by contemporary medicine and science, constructed a model of man that appears to be dynamic, but in essence, is mechanistic: **A** leads to **B**.

The industrial revolution, the railroads, the American Constitution with its three principles, were all conceived as a sophisticated machine with clear and ordered premises - **A** leads to **B**. Even Einstein's physics was essentially mechanistic, although he attributed a place for time. In other words, according to this concept, the scientist is part of the experience, and the experimenter affects the experiment.

Man does not observe a world on which he has no effect; his very presence effects what exists. The investigation of the universe and its basic rules are tied to the investigator himself, or as the tenet goes: "what is seen from here is not seen from there," everything depends on the point of view.

Ilya Prigogine (1984), winner of the 1977 Nobel Prize in Physics for his contribution to the field of thermodynamics, asserted in his book, *Order Out Of Chaos* (1984), that in the mechanistic era following the scientific revolution, certain features were particularly emphasized: stability, order, unity and balance.

Classical science's methodology deals mainly with closed systems and linear relationships which contain small effects that produce minor results.

Conversely, according to the "butterfly effect," the universe is an open system in which small influences can cause revolutionary results. This is the great discovery of the modern era of technology and information compared with mechanistic classical science. Prigogine's research, or what is called The Brussels School, presents an additional breakthrough in this way of thinking. His paradigm draws particular attention to those parts of reality that deal with change, disorder, imbalance, variance, non-linear relationships, (**A** does not necessarily lead to **B**) and temporariness. Its essential concern is to understand the connection between order and chaos in the universe and human society.

According to Prigogine, the fact that reversibility is not possible in the universe or for mankind, it becomes the essential basis of change and progress. In other words, the inability to go backwards stimulates our brain always to invent new solutions.

I shall try to translate this in terms of the human brain as it conceives the world. I mentioned above that learning theories assert that the first learning imprinted in us is negative by nature. For our edification it could be asked: How, if this is so, does every small event seem to be a great one when affecting the infant's learning process? We'll begin with negative learning. The first is learning how to avoid pain. With the passage of time all first learning is changed by processing and sophistication, so that avoidance of physical pain becomes avoidance of mental, social, or existential pain. Because a baby's brain is a formidable receptor, many stimuli accumulate that become translated initially, and are used eventually by the brain center -- known as "self—management." Of these first painful encounters, initially physical and later psychological/social, are formed the initial aversion or "same strategy" of early avoidance, that I have termed the **Impasse.**

Impasse

We have here a fitting example of Prigogine's claim of irreversibility, in other words, inability to reverse to the former situation and thereby create the brain's need to take a new direction. The original pain, a product of the first imprinting, with the addition of necessity, forms the immediate response of flight. But because reverse movement is barred, we have to guide ourselves into a new direction. Thus when the direction is a new one, it will frequently be imprinted as "a pain memory" and the need is for absolute avoidance.

The main argument in understanding the premise of Impasse formation is that it is due to difficult, embarrassing, paralyzing and painful experiences that occurred early in life, and which are linked to the situation that caused them. Thus, these situations become impossible; situations that we won't ever return to voluntarily.

Since we are dealing with the social position of the individual, we must also refer to the response of others in the group to the individual. Even at a tender age the infant cannot deal with a difficult experience logically or protect himself by explanations. He simply utilizes all the experiences of this first negative early learning, and blocks them. The imprinting of negative learning, as we described it, is critical, and thus difficult feelings are handled generally as avoidance; hence the use of the term, Impasse -- NO ENTRY. The grown up adult will even be unaware of having an Impasse.

This lack of awareness is one of the important determinants of treatment.

To summarize this chapter we should consider the following:

1. Negative learning is imprinted stronger than all other types.
2. Marginal events such as the butterfly effect form positions in our brain in early infancy. We no longer follow a single traumatic event, knowing that the brain is being assailed by many stimuli simultaneously, and chooses which one to respond to, and which one will have a traumatic outcome.

THE IMPASSE

The concept "Impasse" is a term derived from the traffic sign standing at the entrance to a road that reads " no through way," or 'cul-de-sac,' or 'no passage.' Theoreticians have proposed many different ideas about first experiences, especially traumatic ones that are imprinted on an individual in early life.

In order to be consistent with my quantum conception, I have to admit that I have no proof that a single universal factor operates as an impassable road or deterrent situation for either children or adults. Ski boarding scares me a lot, as does jumping into the mouth of a volcano. On the other hand, I know people who crave these experiences to satisfy their zest for life. It would be a mistake to think that all infants are alike and that we can identify a general pattern of "parental behavior" that is unconnected to the unique personality of that a parent. Moreover from birth until reaching the tender age of three, we can observe that personality taking shape; personality as opposed to behavior. Behavior is a variable, while personality is the constant kernel that is being formed gradually in the early years.

I don't subscribe to the deterministic school that claims that the shaping of the personality takes place during the so-called "formative years" — until the age of seven. In my system, what is occurring in these early years is the Impasse, and the consequential life strategies which become broader and broader throughout our entire lives. We can ask how does a child choose a direction for itself and at a certain point hangs up a sign saying "no passage." During the process of developing our individual capability, we are seeking a place in human society, a place that will guarantee us a feeling of power and significance, a place that empowers self-expression that accepts and recognizes our existence.[1]

In the process of finding our niche we experience pain, suffering and rejection, which we will later try to avoid. These negative experiences will coalesce to become our Impasse.

The Right to Exist

The very expression "right to exist" implies that a person may feel deprived of this privilege, or that the surrounding world is denying it. We are presently very aware, as we were in the 1930s, that certain powerful nations seek to deny the Jewish people the right to exist. In a similar fashion, not only at the national cultural level but also within small groups, even families, we often find people who aren't sure of their right to exist at all. They feel that this right depends on them meeting certain criteria. Everyone can relate to finding him or herself in a particular social environment that undermines their status or right to exist. Since existence is the essential core of being, it becomes clear that we must prevent, with all our strength, whatever threatens it.

The place of the small child within his family is attended by situations that he perceives as threats to his existence. We are not referring to a physical threat, rather the kind that is universal and shared by everyone. The subjective threat, the negating the possibility of expression, ridicule, immobility and a lack of individuality within the family, are all creators of the Impasse, which is an individual construction and an individual interpretation for each one of us.

The child's interpretation of what is perceived as pain, insult or not being acknowledged for his very existence, undermines the feeling of individuality and value. Take an example from children's drawings. When the child draws himself, his placement on the page is relevant;

sometimes he takes up the whole page, but occasionally the negation of the right to exist is drawn as a tiny figure on a huge page. I would re-emphasize that what we are talking about here is the perception of "no right to exist," or what many adults call "feeling transparent."

The children's fairy tale about the frog waiting to be kissed before turning into a prince, confirms that people believe that without recognition of their existence -- "they don't exist." The Impasse is undoubtedly a feeling of unmet "conditions for existence," or a "lack of recognition" by the world that we are here and we are unique.

At this junction we can consult Prigogine's treatise on brain research and Daniel Siegel's works, for assistance in translating the Impasse in terms of brain activity.

The Brain: Models of Data Processing and Constructing Reality

1. The way by which we experience reality is performed by active tracts of groups of nerve bundles within the brain. Naturally this is an individual and creative activity for each one of us. If this is so, then how do people communicate with one another? How does one brain read the messages sent by a second brain? How are words as well as non-verbal signals of communication, for example, intonation, voice and facial expressions, translated by the brain? How do people "feel appreciated" by others?

2. What is the role of the dominant side of the brain in evaluating reality? For example, do babies and adults whose left brain is developed far better than the right side lack the capacity to "read" others?

The answers to all these questions are related to the fact that the brain is regarded as a machine whose role is to process information. Within this data processing we experience the translation of signs. The signs and symbols received from the outside are processed within the brain where they create new information. This chain of reaction is called "cognitive processing," such as memory and abstract thinking, for example.

In other words, the brain creates symbols whose function is in itself symbolic, and which contains new information. The capacity to process information is inborn, hereditary, while human evolution has required and compelled the brain to specialize in problem solving by exploiting this capacity. Moreover, we should remember that abstract and grandiose concepts, such as freedom or justice, are derived from simple symbolic characters that have been transmuted into a complex program of values.

What is Self-organization?

The central function of the emotions is self-organization. The "self" is formed during the process of the brain's activities for its interaction with the external world. The emotions function as central "organizers and communicators." How does it happen? The emotions organize all the in-coming stimuli within a motivational, targeting framework. It is this complex framework that connects what we characterize as the mental, social and biological aspects.

Self organization of an individual will differ notably in relation to four central traits: intensity, sensitivity, focus and tolerance. As the child develops, these basic emotions become a sophisticated framework, and essentially behavioral categories. The simple emotional polarity of pleasure-pain is translated into fear, anger, shame, curiosity, surprise and joy.

There is increasing evidence that the "conscious ego," in fact represents a small fraction of the brain's activity and its ability to comprehend. The emotional processes, the memory, and especially, the interpersonal relationships, are conducted almost without intervention of consciousness or cognition. The "self," as we stated above, is formed by involuntary processes to the same extent that voluntary ones are formed. Putting it simply, we are "much more" than thinking beings.

What then is the role of cognition in equilibrating the emotions? Its role must surely be to affect the outcome of emotional processing.

The first year of life is characterized by its approach to attachment whereby the infant feels that he is "felt," that his needs are recognized by the parent. The infant expresses its emotions and needs freely, and learns the world's (mother's) reaction to him. In the second year, as the result of this learning, the child knows how and when to show his emotions. A two year old already knows which needs will not be fulfilled, or even worse, which demands will induce an angry response or other negative reactions.

Let us briefly summarize what we now know about PPs from physics and brain research.

1. There are no minor effects; all effects can induce great changes.

2. There are no reversions in data reception; a negative experience is not erased rather it is coerced to organize anew.

3. The self organization of the brain is constructed by translating a myriad of stimuli and signals, unique for each individual. This is the key to personality. Organization of the emotions — especially those responding to positive and negative events— will become the basis of personality, and produce vital strategies that organize themselves according to a central preference or a life strategy.

In order to locate the Impasse we should reemphasize that it is formed within the brain's center for self-management. It is not a thought but an experience that is translated into the level of awareness.

IMPASSE — PSYCHOLOGICAL ASPECTS

Awareness and classification are the rapid instinctive reactions upon meeting new people. When we say, "I know him" — the general intention is our ability to predict this person's action or guess what type of decisions he will adopt. In many cases there is no link between our prediction ("I know him") and what this person will actually do. But we can't forego this process because people are like a landscape and to move along its highways, we need a map.

Our "cognition" is supported by previous experiences instinctively mobilized for this new encounter. Here we have an instinctive recycling of basic responses — "it's nice…" or "it's not nice…," that we translate as perception and reception of the general traits evidenced by the behavior of the other. Sayings such as: "I know this character," "I knew straight away what he would decide," and "I can't bear such characters," or even: "she's charming, I love this type of person," indicate clearly our own life experience rather than that of the person we are describing. We usually describe the visible behavior of the person. It's more difficult to decipher what type of inter-personal bond the other person will avoid at any price, or what he won't do. The concept "Impasse" is the exact inter-personal bond that each one of us will not allow himself to become entrapped, to the extent that it depends on him. This is an interpersonal situation in which we may feel insignificant, rejected, inexperienced or even neutralized. We'll discuss these concepts even though we all probably know their meaning.

In the previous chapter we dealt with the manner that data is processed by the brain during its reception. As we said, the basic response to the brain's reception of information is "I like it /I don't like it," which extends into different, complex and sophisticated forms of responses. "I like it" can also be -- I am important, significant, loved, appreciated, pleased, happy, energetic, want more. "I don't like it" can develop into sad, down, rejected, unimportant, useless, wanting to run away.

The PP, as defined, is a chart of social behavior. Therefore, it's not in the sense of "I don't like it because boiling water has been spilt on me," but "I don't like to be opposite these people in such a situation." We'll start with "I like it" and then with "I don't like it." I will present the basic positive experiences that are needed for the development of the "ego," as well as the negative ones. Both are personal interpretations of interpersonal experiences in early life.

Psychological Components in Human Relationships

Ernest Becker (1973), the 1974 Pulitzer Prize winner and author of *The Denial of Death*, coined a key phrase: Cosmic specialness. Becker claimed that at the root of resolute personality, which is independent and self-confident, can be located the consciousness of the child's and adult's cosmic specialness. According to Becker, the use of the phrase cosmic specialness doesn't belong to the era (the 1960s), but simply to the fact that out of the millions of humans, there are no two who are absolutely identical. Each person has an extra value. In addition to a person's innate traits, he has unique ones. Uniqueness does not develop *de novo*. In early life someone, usually the mother, or someone close, recognizes the cosmic specialness of the infant.

If, for example, we look at a young mother hovering over her baby, we can see that she is overjoyed at the sight of the wonderful being reclining in the crib. It has a certain something that captures her heart, a something that stimulates a special response, a response that no other person can elicit in her. While we, who also want to be enchanted with the scenario, peep into the crib and sometimes see "a little monkey" lying there. What does the mother see that we can't? This "miracle" happening to this baby can or will happen to him several times in a lifetime, and can happen to all of us. The significance of the "miracle" is that "someone sees something in me," which enables me to "feel felt."

The world of art is rich in stories of people who no one believed in, until the "master" arrives, points to the student, and says: "He has it." A second grade teacher can also significantly affect a child's life, when she sees something in the child that no other sees. It also happens when we fall in love, and if we are lucky, the loved one also loves us. People in love can always see in one another something that no one else sees. You often hear people saying, "only God knows what they've found in each other."

During the early years of life children will observe something special in their parent, and as we well know they will get over it! But at least the parent is engulfed in incomparable pleasure at the beginning, which gives a feeling of singularity, specialness and significance. Of course in every group there are only a few who through their lives are seen as having cosmic specialness, or charisma, which in Greek means 'God's gift.'

It is important to understand this term correctly. In cosmic specialness, there is no intention of a universal contribution to the world, and there is no significant connection with behavior. When we identify a unique property in other persons, it means simply that we too are affected, that we externalize ourselves for a moment in order to see it, that something in this encounter awakens an emotion within our brain and sweeps us away momentarily.

In an argument with an American colleague concerning Becker's message, my colleague claimed that people who can be identified by others as being special, are fortunate. In contrast, I thought that the ability to recognize others as special was in itself unique, and usually people don't bother about it. In the sphere of education and the world of therapy, recognition of the specialness in someone is a vital condition.

I have been asked many times if the most insipid character has cosmic specialness. Today, after many long years of work, I can say with certainty that the answer is yes, but I also know there are springs that burst forth unaided, and there is dark and deep water that can be reached only by drilling.

Let us talk once more about early childhood and the feeling that someone knows you and allows you to be "you," as distinct from everyone else. This is not because of any specific skills that were prominent in childhood. Rather this is an undefined recognition which originates in the right brain, and not in analytical thought. Becker linked this recognition with self-confidence, with an unconscious wish to develop uniqueness that we ourselves are incapable of defining.

Do all children become recognized for their specialness? Of course not. As far as it concerns us here, it is enough to say that children will repeat those behaviors or situations where they are rewarded for their specialness. These rewards constitute an acknowledgment of their existence as independent individuals, and they will avoid situations where they are not recognized at all.

In those early years the child's personal commentary is critical. His self-organization and ability to recognize situations that are good for him, and others that aren't good. These are the foundation building blocks of the personality. In summary, we emphasize those situations where the child is unrecognized, feels unfelt or non-existing and which are responsible for forming the Impasse.

Reference Groups

According to Becker, the identification of cosmic specialness is related principally to the mother and through her to the family. If the child does not get this recognition in his early years, he can still be discovered in later years, by teachers, by falling in love or through achievements.

In these early years the child looks into many mirrors, and responds to many groups of people from whom he gets different reactions. "I like it" or "I don't like it" is experienced differently from each group. The basic need for recognition of our existence, our separateness, our special experiences — will differ from group to group.

All of us will easily recognize that we relate to other people according to a set of rules that has not been accorded much importance previously. Recognizing those rules, is most important to our understanding of the Impasse.

We experience people by unconsciously dividing them into three groups:

1. The authoritative group
2. The peer group
3. The dependant group

The Authoritative Group

This is the first group of people that we encounter in the world. These are the parents, the nursemaids, grandparents, the kindergarten staff, and all the adults that surround the infant in his first years. This group, with its different responsibilities, takes charge of the child's existence, survival, its health, and contented growth.

In the early years social behavior is critically learned through this group. We comply, completely submitting ourselves, developing expectations and wishes, while learning and identifying ourselves only with this group. Our first learning will take place here during the socialization process; we learn how people inter-behave. We are still aware that this formula of the child and responsible adult is about to widen, and we are about to be exposed to two more groups of people that include the rest of the adult generation: teachers, supervisors, leaders, dignitaries, representatives of law and order (these too are appointed by this group), and the state itself. Eventually we will see that our relationship in infancy with this group fills an important role that determines how we are situated in the future towards members of this group.

At the two extremes we find those who trust and respect people within the authoritative groups, as opposed to those who are suspicious of authority - whether it resides in a single person, an organization (the school or army, for example) or the local or national government.

The little child encounters his parents, who are closest to him, in this group. He sees them as his support and road map and who are aware of his existence, and who endorse him. The child not only needs training from them but also the support and approval of this group. Sometimes the authoritative group doesn't play its part. Occasionally a reversal of roles occurs, with the child relying on himself rather than on his parents. This can lead to an uncertainty occurring in his relationship with authority.

When the child respects and accepts the authority in the early years, it will probably continue throughout his life. The authoritative group represents the universal order, nature's hierarchy, and even the rules of law and order.

Routine identification with this group will eventually lead to adopting authority and becoming a member of the authority group. The sequence of development is child to adult to parent, and thus the future parent is based in the child. The idea is obviously that a parent is an adult person who will extend his authority beyond himself to his children, pupils, employees, and the world.

The identifying motto of the authoritative group is responsibility.

The Peer Group

Alfred Adler's important contribution to personality development puts special emphasis on the peer groups in the family. According to his approach, the struggle is to establish a place among the family peer group of siblings and what is requisite is to be different from the others in order to be acknowledged, "to feel felt." This rule is generally operative for an age difference of seven years, and it outlines the future life style. Starting with the first move from home to the kindergarten, and throughout many years at school, the child may find himself at odds with the sibling group. Generally it transpires that the child's place among his brethren will also reflect his primary role in the sibling group.

Whereas in other groups the child's role is obvious (viz., bigger than or smaller than), in the peer group he is expected to construct his own place. The process of socialization with its various stages empowers his finding his place in this group, and while the authoritative and the dependant groups always remain the same, the sibling or peer group itself changes.

Up until the ages of 18 - 21 this group generally includes his peers, classmates, teammates, and club mates. But the adult is multi-affiliate, and the equal group, will broaden to include people in the same professions, neighborhood and work place, and those who share the same pastimes. Or there will be people from many other age groups and activities, and what makes them equal groups will usually be a single common denominator.

Three groups in an adult's life are determined by the person himself after the imprinting of the first impressions, while the first sensations of "nice" and "not nice" are related to his belonging to and his position in each group. As one's repertoire of behavior widens, a person will feel comfortable with all groups and can interact eye to eye without feeling inferior and without arrogance. In my clinical experience I have found that most people tend to feel less affiliated with one of the three groups but feel at ease with the other two.

In an attempt to find a person's first priority, it is very important to ascertain to which of the groups he attributes importance, to which group he wishes to belong, and with whom he has a primary difficulty in making a connection. I have found that most people when introduced to the idea of the three groups reacted as though they had never contemplated such a possibility. However, once the subject was presented, there was no one who couldn't reply or describe his problems with the world, in terms of this concept.

The important implications of these groups will, of course, be in marriage, parenthood and integrating into the work life. In correlation with the division into groups we can also consider political leanings, being either identification or revolt.

Despite the fact that at any particular moment we are surrounded by people belonging to any of the three groups, and we ourselves are identified by others as belonging to one or another group, nevertheless our response is not uniform.

Most people, as stated earlier, feel comfortable with at least two groups, while the third is more difficult for them to adapt to. Some people make an effort to be mainly with one group while there are those who specifically "erase" one group. These are, of course, due to their early childhood imprinting. We are referring to a feeling rather than necessarily a behavior. For example, not accepting the authoritative group could be concealed by the individual, for practical reasons, especially as authority denotes social hierarchy, the state, the law, entrance examinations, etc.

A person can be hostile towards the authoritative group and insist all through life that being in its presence is like being in an "enemy camp." Another person regards the authoritative group as a support, a route for promotion, or something to lean on and be helped by. Our encounter with people who represent one of these groups makes us feel immediately, "nice" or "not nice," "worth my time" or "not worth my time," "I can be significant" or "I haven't a chance with this group."

The Dependant Group

In describing the dependant groups, there is no evaluative criterion, rather descriptions of its members includes those who are younger and smaller than us — age-wise and position-wise. In childhood, this group may include objects and animals since the child derives a feeling of control from this group. This strength will eventually become responsibility.

A small child depends on the wishes of others regarding fulfillment of his needs, but he finds out that there are those who are even more dependent, for example his toys, as well as his younger brother, newborn and helpless. This may generate, a new feeling of strength that he experiences for the first time.

An example: When a four-year-old girl is playing with her doll and imitating her mother, we see a direct transference. The child knows how to talk to someone her junior, who depends on her. She tells her what and what not to say, even gives her a smack and says, "No, no, no," hugs and kisses her, and repeats the terms of affection she hears from her own mother.

Early on, a child discovers a new power over his younger siblings. Some children find that power is a way to control, while others assume a responsible role. Encounters with the authoritative group are unavoidable because they are present and active from birth.

It is also possible that a child will not relate to the dependent group at all. A good example is the only child, or the youngest family members. Many children in this group relate to their elders as the only reference group since it is the only one they know, respect and rely on. For them the other two groups are optional, and we frequently see people who never relate to their juniors or peers in a significant way. This behavior can be explained by a lack of experience or identifying figure from the other groups. Once the child identifies authority and acknowledges it, he himself becomes authoritative — and responsible for his juniors.

Those who don't have any appreciation for their juniors in their behavioral repertoire, usually continue to relate primarily to the authoritative group. A younger brother who steals the show can also bring about a suspension of relations, or present a threat for their group. We can also find those children who can relate to their juniors, and who feel at ease and have meaning specifically with their juniors, but not with their own age group — for them this is a peer group.

"The Enemy Camp"

At the beginning of the twentieth century, Freud coined the term neurosis in the context of an agitation, or more precisely as a "defensive behavior." According to Freud, neurosis characterizes a person whose behavior is based on anxiety, and a consequence, seeks to protect himself all his life from an unknown and uncontrolled threat.

Adler, in his socially-based psychology, defined neurosis as anxiety with a societal origin. He described the neurotic person as one living in an "enemy camp." The concept of "enemy camp" is an abstract one, so I have tried to create a certain model to explain it. Firstly, who is prepared to live in an "enemy camp?"

The example I use here is the spy. A spy immerses himself in an enemy camp where he works, makes friends, and behaves as if this was his home. His behavior doesn't convey in any way his inner life. While he is living like everyone else, three basic assumptions guide him all the time.

1. If all these people, with whom I am living, knew the truth about me, I would die.

2. To prevent this from happening, I must not make a single error. Every error can be fatal - therefore I must continually be on guard.

3. This life is so tense and dangerous but it will end when the "contract' ends, and then my "real life" will begin.

These three presumptions create suspicion, an inability to become really close, perfectionism, and a feeling of impermanence. This is a defensive life, and every one in his vicinity is a potential enemy. There's no need to be a spy living in an enemy camp in order to experience these states; many who live normal lives in their countries and homes, and also feel this way.

The Transition from the Impasse to Construction of an Inter-personal Life Strategy

The Impasse as described differs from person to person, and can be divided into four categories that include those situations that people avoid routinely.

The Impasse, derived from negative basic experiences, presents a foundation on which to build a strategic-behavioral platform that includes everything concerning human relations and our place on earth. This behavioral strategy, constructed on avoidance, becomes the basic preference for one's personal behavior. I have called this the Personality Priority (PP) to help us understand the sense of a perpetual search by the personality to achieve the feeling of acceptance, value and meaning.

Behavior is a tool for acquiring a place in the world that satisfies our quest for those desired feelings. I have identified four types of Impasses that in turn represent the basis of four classes of behavior and preferential behavioral strategies.

Impasse No. 1 - A feeling of insignificance — strategy or Personality Priority - Superiority

Impasse No. 2 - A feeling of rejection - strategy or Personality Priority — Pleasing

Impasse No. 3 - A feeling of uselessness — strategy or Personality Priority - Control

Impasse No. 4 - A feeling of being controlled — strategy or Personality Priority — Avoidance

This strategy becomes our personal achievement, created by the need to fill what was unfulfilled in our childhood. People are doubtful about the achievement, and generally invest in the Priority much creativeness, adjustment, and a feeling of satisfaction.

- Over many years of clinical work on the subject, I have reached several conclusions:

  1. The vast majority of people are unaware of the fact that they return constantly to a single inter- personal behavior model.

  2. The need for satisfaction from the Priority or avoidance of the Impasse becomes a life-long strategy: this isn't an achievable aim but a means to an end. As there is no way to reach the horizon — so too are our life's aims; they are landmarks for progress and perpetual movement without a finish line. This is what the Sages intended when they said: *"No one leaves the world with his wishes half- fulfilled."*

  3. The opportunities for change are in effect the broadening of the behavioral repertoire, but rarely does the Impasse get cancelled or changed.

Everyone behaves according to his current needs and they can identify themselves within all four Priorities. We all use many strategies but only one stands out for us, and we direct ourselves to this. The dominate Priority becomes an important tool in our hands. The satisfaction we derive from this strategy rewards us and gives us our strength.

The tables at the end of the book set out the four Priorities and the Impasses, and include the price that is paid for preferring a single source of power. Similarly they include the attendant restrictions, and the responses of the others. The last column includes goals for improvement. Improvement includes a broadening of the behavioral range and a reduction in the avoidance of the Impasse.

Inferiority

The concept known as the inferiority complex is another of Adler's contribution to an understanding of the basic personality complex. Adler described the development of the personality throughout life as a perpetual mobile — moving from minus to plus swings. The plus will also become minus the moment we reach it, but we continue. According to Adler, the striving for superiority is an ongoing driving force to overcome imperfection is life's basic motive.

We include the inferiority complex as an additional example of the situation of "not nice," that we want to escape from.

Our primary inferiority from birth is a fact. This is demonstrated by the inability of the newborn to sustain himself and his total dependence on others during the long period of development In comparison to the animal kingdom. According to Adler, together with the infant's objective inferiority experienced in his first years, is also a personal inferiority, an awareness and feeling of inferiority within the social matrix in which he grows and develops. The growing but immature child identifies panic signals, physical and social, that he has trouble handling. Within a healthy social network, the child strives to overcome the inferiority by compensatory activity in the source or another area. For example, the child who is a social outsider can become an outstanding student, and there are many accounts of children with visual or hearing inadequacies who become artists and musicians.

According to Adler, it is easier to understand a person if we identify his over-compensation, i.e., his strong side, the abilities he develops to gets ahead. Thus, we have introduced several aspects of the development of the Impasse.

It's important to stress that A doesn't cause B. Life goes on simultaneously with many factors, incidents and feelings at play. We love to be with people who recognize our uniqueness, bestow significance on us, and to belong to a group where we feel important. We avoid people and groups that arouse our feeling of inferiority or a situation of "enemy camp."

As we get older the collection of such situations, variable as they are, become focused and encapsulated symbolically. Each of these situations forms a road sign that we can recognize and that is personal and unique. What a sign or symbol means for one person, could be different or opposite for others.

This commentary, authentic and symbolic, is, of course, subjective. When we tell a friend about a third person, that he is unbearable, and the friend questions "What do you mean? He's really nice," this isn't meant to be a comment about the third person, rather it expresses our attitude, or our obligation to avoid "not nice" in all its forms.

While I was developing my PP model I regarded the Impasse as a foremost concept. At the start, like an infant, we recognize what does not work for us in our personal relations, and we shut this route down. This resembles the road with a sign warning us of a hazard further on. There are people who will travel to this hazard and then halt, and there are others who won't even approach it. The situations that we avoid are those, where we aren't significant — we feel down, and feel unable to exert our strength. We hold back using various degrees of avoidance. Each individual's response depends on his life experiences, the ability to identify situations, and our speed of response.

Self-management and the Formation of the Impasse

Is the Impasse formed as a process, a collection of negative experiences, or just formed instantaneously? Our answer is helped by "the butterfly effect," and the understanding that even a marginal effect can somehow gain momentum and sweep in its path additional experiences of a similar nature and thus become our Impasse. Often during therapy, people will tell me the worst experience in their lives was a ban imposed on them in the third grade. This only lasted for a day, but was never forgotten. Others relate when the second grade teacher asked a question, they put up their hand and answered correctly, but all the class broke into laughter. Do these situations necessarily produce the Impasse? I don't think so. After decades of experience, which formed the basis of my PP system, I have concluded that the Impasse is created at a much younger age, at a stage when we do not even remember and cannot retrieve early memories.

In this connection I would like to refer to Arthur Janov's controversial book, *The Primal Scream* (1983). Janov, who was a student of the psychoanalytic school, argued with Freud's basic concept regarding the primary trauma in a child's life. Freud interpreted the primary trauma as a significant influence on the emerging personality, but he pointed to several life events of equal importance and universal for everybody. A good example was the Oedipus complex and its repression.

Janov argued that early traumas that are "contracted" events, not universal, are subjective to various degrees. His example of a slamming door that causes great panic for one child while another remains impassive, illustrates how differently common events affect us as a child and the child's subjective response to it.

Janov gives the example of a three-year-old boy, an only child, adored, the center of his parents' life, confident of his place and importance in the world. One day he over-hears his mother talking on the phone to a friend: "This weekend the two of us, by ourselves, are finally getting away — I'm so looking forward to it." Janov lists six types of children and their reactions or passivity to what they heard. One of the six, at that moment, changes his concept of his status in the house (and in the world). "Ah, they no longer really love me, they want to get away from me." He won't remember this event, nor will his mother, but the information feeds into his self-management center, his world view, and ultimately his behavior. A trauma has occurred. Janov points to the "self-management" of the child and sees there the formation of the self.

Anxiety of the Self

Let us reconsider the basic concepts on which we seldom linger. What is subject anxiety? Most terms have an objective connotation. An example: On a certain day the temperature is 15 degrees Celsius outside. In Tel Aviv this is a cold day. Does everyone feel cold? No, and there are even people who are sweating. How can we determine that this is indeed a cold day?

The objectivity, or whatever is measurable, or what common sense tells us, will always differ from personal sensations. Our feelings, or our private logic, always deviate somewhat from the common sense. Our private logic and common sense rarely completely harmonize.

From the time a child (ages 7-12) begins to show separation from his primary, family circle, he runs into criticism, even outright rejection of his opinion. It takes a lot of guts to develop a personal, and therefore a subjective "self authority," and also express it. In some homes no freedom of expression is allowed, only so-called "objectivity" which is, the adult's opinion of what is "correct" or "not correct" about everything. One child will swallow his opinions, a second will freely express them.

In the process of the subjective development of our private logic and personal feelings — we are in danger of opposition or "engulfment." Most of the important decisions in our lives are subjective – what we eat, dress, learn, and who we marry. Drawing on our personal "center of inner authority," we often try to make "objective" decisions in answer to subjective questions. Take for example the question "to marry her or not?" We diligently make an "objective" list for and against, which is inherently subjective, and hardly ever leads to a resolution. Part of the individual's personal uniqueness is this inner "center of authority." The Chinese define it as "the unknown knowledge," which is a clear understanding, that is not directly based on knowledge but on an inner feeling of security that confirms our subjective opinions, our choices, decisions, and innermost inclinations.

The Impasse is formed subjectively, by means of a unique, non-verbal commentary of inter-personal experiences, which is what happens to us in our human relationships.

To sum up the formation of a behavioral strategy is not target-orientated but avoidance-orientated. The first social sign of our place in the world is indirect, created by distancing ourselves from painful experiences. Because these are early imprintings, we are unaware of our instinctive flinching from pain and the way that pain avoidance affects the fundamentals of our behavior and social interactions.

THE SUPERIOR

Rabban Shimon ben Gamliel says: *On three things the world stands; on truth, on judgment, and on peace…* (*Ethics of the Fathers*).

When I first introduced the Priorities I called superiority "Moral Superiority." Over the years I have encountered numerous responses ranging from a raised eyebrow to open criticism, to simple misunderstanding about the term. For this reason I renamed it "Superiority." Like Adler's term "Striving for Superiority," which is also incorrectly understood, the term superiority is interpretable as exclusive, or lofty, or even aloof towards others.

I would emphasize that the use of the term is purely and simply directed to the power of personal motivation, to a continuous drive to significance. If there is any aloofness here it is opposite to what is usually thought. This person has no need for the praise of others; he is his own judge, sometimes to the extent of denying the group, which in itself could be termed aloofness.

While I was working on this book, the Israel Defense Force engaged in an operation to return the casualties and 200 bodies to the Hezbollah. My surprise was complete when I heard on the radio that the operation was called "Moral Superiority." Like the categorization into individual types, nations and cultures are similarly subdivided. It is clear that Judaism is a culture of "Moral Superiority," and thus the name of the operation whose aim was solely humanitarian and whose price was painfully high.

Basic Traumatic Experiences – Impasse

If we relate to negative experiences, nations are characterized by the same life strategies. There is no description more concise than the Jewish ethos "You chose us," the cosmic specialness which is our mythological peculiarity is our ultimate value. Impasses that are substantiated by "Remember that which...." Why remember? Because we don't remember. Even the national Impasse is no longer remembered but is deeply imprinted. It is so for man and for the nation.

The flood of first negative experiences consists of all those situations that the child interprets as indefinite, with regard to his position in the family. The developing feeling is: I am insignificant, lacking specialness, unidentified, don't belong, no one has discovered me, other family members are significant, there is something about me that doesn't warrant attention, I am transparent.

As we recall, this isn't a solitary event but a continuous feeling. These feelings of worthlessness within a family will occur mostly in those families where the concept of significance and uniqueness exist. Someone is a "victim" because of his dedication, someone else is worth more, and generally there are people who are more equal than others. There are both "better" and "lesser." Often the whole family regards itself as "worth more" within the community, except for the child who has not yet acquired the skills that make him "worth more."

In such a family, if you aren't "worth more," then you are "worthless." These are all abstract concepts. The child still doesn't know what is required of him to be special, but he senses the family atmosphere. This, of course, is a primary sensation, muffled, unclear, but it has imprinted its seal and requires consideration.

Often the "special ones" in the family don't stand out as anything special, and they exploit their suffering as victims; a kind of "the world doesn't grant me what I deserve." The rest of the family may also live with this social "victimization," even though it's not clear what they "deserve." A wise man once said: "My biography doesn't suite me." This is laughable because our biography indeed suits us. It is us. However, many people in this world go through life with a feeling that "I deserve more."

In other words, the home or the mother, who didn't get sufficient meaning in the world, very often finds it difficult to be givers of meaning. The mother can be devoted, rear her children, work hard, spare herself, and sacrifice herself, but one thing is beyond her ability: Due to her marked preoccupation with her own worth, she can't bestow meaning on her fellow-man.

I started with this Impasse, perhaps because it is really hard to understand. This is an abstract difficulty, like the concept of "meaning" is abstract. I have yet to meet the person who on hearing the word "meaning" will ask "what's that?" The person, who is unable to define the concept in words, understands it, feels it, is excited by it. The child, in this case, should be intelligent and deprived, because he feels this deprivation in the abstract sense, a deprivation that is not connected to his immediate needs. Many children, who are protected and contented, are not bothered at all with meaning.

Meaning is not something that we expect from our fellow man, just as we cannot ask someone to be enthralled with what we say. We can expect an audience, but whether the audience is captivated or not, is a natural consequence.

Will all the children in this family feel the same? Not necessarily. There can be one child who enjoys immediate satisfaction, is productive, sensual, social, with a positive outlook, and has no interest in being "special."

Emphasis on suffering is one aspect of the superiority feeling that predicts particularly a sense of sacrifice and denial. As a contrast, I can give an example of an additional type, a representative of an achieving family where achievement is an ultra-objective. Achievements are connected with doing and satisfaction which is in itself doing, being the functional development of capabilities, and revealing that every person has the possibility of achieving his aims. The pursuit of excellence would tend to endow a person with an image of excellence, even if he has not yet achieved it. Here there is a feeling of superiority that is connected to ambition and an actual drive for achievement.

For example, we know many people who can manage, are satisfied, with just being average. As another example, families may boast about their ancestors who achieved their status independently. The present generation would boast their connections and value on the basis of being born into this family.

A lot has been written about the need for uniqueness, and I have often seen that uniqueness can be oppositional to that of belonging. Sociologists define this polarity as reference groups as opposed to membership groups.

Another model of superiority is a feeling of uniqueness. A feeling of superiority isn't necessarily connected to achievements; it can be based on a general feeling of uniqueness. For example, a family living in a poor neighborhood may regard their circumstance as a temporary situation. The children are brought up with a feeling of not belonging to the ambient environment; they are raised to belong to a reference group that they don't even know, a virtual group that dresses differently, speaks differently and aspires to other values. The feeling of belonging to something unrecognized is expressed principally as not belonging to what surrounds you, as opposed to where you really belong. Energy is directed at emphasizing the difference, without a practical model for positive belonging.

What can be the causative factor for the formation of an Impasse stemming from a lack of significance for one child, and not for another? One component is the child's attitude to one of three groups: the authoritative group, the peer group and the dependant group. The child who "seeks significance" has an attitude that identifies particularly to the authoritative group, which he wants to copy and acquire its perceived rewards. He is intelligent, self-demanding and is never satisfied with his achievements. Another child doesn't view the authoritative group as a source for imitation, and he expects that this group will provide his needs. This child who doesn't "feel felt," tries all his life to escape from this situation; he will identify it immediately, and its avoidance will become the keystone in building a different life strategy.

The child who doesn't feel felt will experience two parallel processes as an adult: In one – he will adapt to his situation, and under certain circumstance in his life, prefer to be anonymous and not felt (internally he always feels not felt). Secondly – and in parallel – he will always compensate himself with certain interests and locations, where he will be significant, contribute, be outstanding and special. The world's response won't change the feeling of anonymity that accompanies his life, there will always be the need to be outstanding, to contribute more, and be felt.

The Existential Condition and Life's Strategy – The Priority

The title "Moral Superiority" was determined from the outset, as was the need to explain it immediately. My intention by the concept of superiority is to require **more effort**, not necessarily superior as opposed to inferior. The "more" is an aim that stimulates an active, unfinished process. What is moral aspect? What is to be worth more? We talked about "the right to exist" that isn't everyone's right. By this priority, a man creates for himself the existential condition – he has the right to exist only if he is worthy, contributes and is responsible.

It is clear that these are all abstract wishes that elegantly skip over the material needs of existence: money, good time, comfort, recreation – compared with an inner feeling of satisfaction that is abstract.

Man sees himself as deriving inspiration from the authoritative group and passing it on to the junior group. World enrichment is essential for him as much as self-enrichment is conditional to his existence. In his opinion not to be felt or to be a "nobody" is a state of basic inferiority. We might emphasize that this man could be a great achiever, but he views himself as "insufficient."

In advancing this theory I was helped by Adler's basic idea concerning the theme of "inferiority" that leads to "over- compensation." The personality which develops from a minus to a plus situation, tends to compensate itself specifically in the same field. Adler found that in his studies on children who were "neighborhood victims," many of them became "professional boxers." Children with weak hands became pianists, and there are many more examples of an inferior status becoming the flag ship. Adler (1907) in his book *Organ Inferiority & its Psychical Compensations* examined the subject extensively. The doctrine of priorities deals mainly with socialization, or establishing the child's place in the world. The Priority, or the life strategy of a child "lacking significance," will turn out to be "significance at any price."

As has already been stated above, there is no single, central factor that becomes the organizing principle of the personality; whether it is physical inferiority, social, the family constellation, the economic situation and dozens of other factors – all of these influences. The child gathers, interprets, and turns them into universal concepts of which he, himself is central.

Recall Abraham Maslow's unique work in designing man's pyramid of needs. At the broad base of the pyramid are the basic needs, while at the apex Maslow placed the "higher needs" among which was the need to feel influential. I think that there is a complementary relationship between Frankl's concept of significance and Maslow's necessity to influence. Influence is not power, at least not in a physical sense. A dictator can influence through fear, but this fear carries the threat of pain and violence and can impact the behavior of large groups and nations. However, the ability to influence or inspire, is mainly spiritual, because it stimulates the other's thinking and actions voluntarily and not through blind obedience. Influence is a stimulus and in Maslow's words, everyone has a need to feel influential.

In early life we are influenced continuously and consequently, we learn the process well. The effect is the opposite of passivity, it requires involvement, or according to Maslow's concept – a kind of altruism. Both a negative influence and bad usage of the ability to influence are obviously possible; moreover, the need to feel influential is basically identical to the need to feel significant.

Life's Strategy and its Practical Expression

The search for significance resembles journeying to the North Star, similarly to "You will see the Promised Land but you won't reach it." Significance is not a conceptual aim but a way of life. There are people who chose another route to achieve significance, such as self-sacrifice or simply the feeling that they know what has to be done.

The superior always feels under duress, fatigued, "over-responsible," and experiences asymmetrical relationships. He also believes he always gives more than he receives. Failure to receive becomes a trait, while independence from your fellowman becomes a way of life. Deep down is a feeling that no one really cares about him.

A paradox is formed: A person seeking significance for his existence gets it from his fellowman, but does not actually need the fellowman himself. Our hero cannot derive a feeling of certainty from any relationship, and in effect he feels alone. His aloneness is not isolation: he is continually surrounded by people, but the feeling of aloneness is existential.

In the end, this person believes in the complex and sad side of life rather than the happy go lucky one, sees the distance and not only what is at hand. Abstract ideas become personal, and they are always more challenging than immediate needs. So the capacity for closeness is expressed as "closeness from a distance." This person cannot survive in a symbiotic close relationship. He must protect his uniqueness, his breathing space and distance.

When we conceptualize the life strategies or Priority we are generalizing. Obviously the individual's biographical background, intelligence, physical and many others characteristics will be important in themselves, at the level and direction that the individual chooses.

In my view the generalization will resemble an aerial photograph – the main routes are visible, and the individual's objective determines the direction of the movement. The person that we are defining here in terms of socialization strives for an ultimate meaning – he will succeed or fail based on many factors and multiple abilities; however this is the direction of the traffic, or his map of the world.

Superiority is the strategic target; and even though unachievable, it becomes the preeminent drive for the person's style of action in this world. This is the source of the Priority concept. The aim, achieving significance, gains priority over other forms of behavior. The imperative to contribute and connect between the right to exist and the feeling of belonging presents difficult limitations for the person. In order to feel special it is essential to observe those surrounding us, identifying what is shared by all while emphasizing our difference. In other words, we don't belong. Belonging may exist in a more abstract mode.

Adler defined belonging as an expression of the need to contribute to the group from a position of equality. However, the person, who develops the need to be different and special, views belonging to a group a situation that blurs his identity, a kind of assimilation. For many people not belonging or being different presents an alternative approach to molding the personality. This is so since every person possesses something special, or according to Becker – cosmic specialness.

The quest for significance nullifies the dependency on life's pleasures. And what are "life's pleasures?" How do they differ from satisfaction? Satisfaction is a feeling connected with a certain achievement, while pleasure is unconnected with activity. The latter is an existential situation; relaxation, at rest with oneself, concentrating on what you are doing now. Once while walking down a street, I passed by a hummus stand. A man sitting there was totally engaged in "wiping up" the hummus on his plate, he was so immersed in his hummus, that the sensual delight was also smeared on his face, like the hummus. He wasn't aware of anybody, he didn't "raise an antenna" to perceive how he was being perceived at that instant. It was just him, the hummus and the pita bread. What pleasure! While observing him I discovered something else: He stimulated my appetite for a plate of hummus on the spot, despite my dislike for this dish. His pleasure, like all delights, stimulates desire.

Pleasure is also the ability to burst into laughter. To hear the first line of a familiar "stand up" routine, and immediately double up with uncontrollable laughter – like the hummus wiper, not at all concerned with how he looks. He is simply enjoying himself, happy, living in the moment. Although I have mentioned two kinds of pleasure – sensual (a good wine) and physical (the humor), the capacity to immerse oneself in such a situation is in itself a delight.

Our individual, who out of necessity has taken it on himself always to be significant, has trouble to just enjoy himself. There is an element of asceticism here, especially where it concerns the senses. How does he enjoy himself? His pleasures are abstract derived for example in thinking, in presenting an idea, in solving a problem, in anonymous philanthropy, and in operating behind the scenes.

His immediate circle feels a certain ambivalence towards him. On the one hand, they respect or even admire him, attempting to seek his help, relying on him, treating him as a source of inspiration. And on the other hand, they feel disappointment because he doesn't need them. Another disappointment is their inability to influence him. It's like a one-way street – you are affected by him, but you don't feel effectual. And our hero, what affects him?

It is usually abstract ideas stimulated by parents, teachers, writers, scientists, philosophers, etc. These are vertical relations not horizontal ones.

Attitude toward Time

It is important to mention the connection between significance and its place in time. At any specific moment we live in the present, aware of the past and with a vision into the future. However, people differ in their individual postures of each of these times. For example, Jewish culture is concerned with the past. All the noteworthy events have already taken place, from Mount Sinai to the Holocaust, and we are obliged to them. American culture is future-orientated; the concepts of progress and change are fundamental, and the South American culture is one of the present. The future (*manyana*) is abstract. Significance never belongs to the present; there is a past significance and a future significance. The present time is free of significance. We noted earlier that Viktor Frankl regarded significance as a continuous, abstract search that is devoid of any realistic experience in the present.

Therapy

Usually, when the Superior comes for treatment, it is based on several possible reasons:

1. A need for self-awareness – a form of learning and a procedure to improvement.

2. Isolation – a difficulty in appreciating the feeling of aloneness despite his over-involvement.

3. Overwork, fatigue, a feeling of bitterness about the universal asymmetry of give and take.

This person will choose his therapist, and will want to be convinced that the therapist is worthy. The role and the qualifications don't affect him, he needs to identify the "specialness" of the therapist and be sure that it will be a mutual procedure.

These days it is common to talk about "philosophical treatment." In my opinion all treatment is philosophical, especially in one aspect: each person has his life, and his own version of his life.

We don't have the capacity to change a person's life only his version of it. A change in concept, which stems from new information at the center for self-management in the brain, this and only this, can bring about a change.

However, we must remember that acquiescence with whom we are, recognizing our shortcomings and taking advantage of our good points are in itself, a change. For many people this is the greatest change.

Summary

The aspiration for superiority presents a fixed motive in this person's life. There is no chance for an experience or a feeling of contentment, since aspiration itself has become an on-going motivation. However, this ambition creates interest, curiosity and study; in effect it never ceases to exist but is always changing its shape.

THE PLEASER

Rabban Hanania ben Dosa says: *"With whom the people are content, so also is God"* (Ethics of the Fathers).

In the previous chapter we dealt with moral superiority and defined the Impasse as an abstract feeling of insignificance, typical of a child who hasn't "been discovered."

Now we'll deal with another child. The basic inferiority of the Pleaser child isn't abstract but very grounded. He fails in his responsibilities. When the responsibilities are studies he has much difficulty in concentration, practice, and lacks willingness to make a mental or Sisyphean effort, such as doing homework or continued concentration in class. This child doesn't like to help with housework, work in the garden, help father fix the tap, or look after his younger siblings. All forms of work bore him and make him feel tired, so he doesn't succeed.

Often hyper-active people wind up included in this category, as well as people with learning disabilities, and attention-deficit problems. All these will be the basis for the development of the Impasse.

It is important to remember that no person or child will tolerate a position of inferiority without over-compensating in one way or another.

For example, children with learning difficulties, in many cases, can be compared to a "blockage of the plumbing," which doesn't include in any way shortcomings in intelligence. On the contrary, we recall that we are aided here by the example of the hyper-active child who quickly discovers his limitations. He becomes impatient, and what is not grasped immediately – is not grasped. Life is hard work from which he is trying to escape since his birth. He isn't aware of the reason or source of his difficulties - with obeying, being quiet, his inability to complete the job, or to fulfill his promises. From an early age he is condemned to the fact that his background is trying to rein in his temperament, to inhibit him, to train him.

While we are aided here by examples such as learning difficulties, we shouldn't forget that the Impasse is created in early life, in the pre-conscious, pre-school and pre-kindergarten period. The infant is aware and interprets his inability to obey, to learn from his parents, to hone in on the project. He experiences innumerable negative experiences in his attempt "to do things," even before he registers that others managed to do them. He absorbs criticism and experiences dissatisfaction from the way he manages himself, by his "idleness," the need to please himself instead of "progressing," and he begins to see the world opposing his life's pleasures.

The first criticism that he is aware of is a mixture of rejection and ridicule. The ridicule is linked to his faulty improvisations regarding tasks, jobs, endeavors and seriousness. The criticism is interpreted as rejection. We stated earlier that all inferiority feelings generate compensation. If this is so, how does a person compensate himself for rejection?

Everyone experiences rejection, and it is a difficult feeling that no one enjoys. However the state of being rejected has two levels. One is factual – that you were unwanted and told so personally to your face. The second is the feeling of rejection that is not necessarily real. Many times the anticipation of acceptance or popularity is so strong, that passive, unenthusiastic acceptance is interpreted as rejection. When you expect longingly to be a sensation, or at least to be accepted with joy, but encounter passivity, it is perceived as rejection or abandonment. The impediment is that longing to receive confirmation of your existence, that you really feel needed, becomes elevated as a condition for endorsing your place in the world. This need for the response of others to enhance your feeling of legitimacy and existence creates a trap.

Traumatic Basic Experiences – Impasse

The state of being valueless turns into a feeling of major inferiority. As a child growing up there is a feeling of derision. As an adult, the Pleaser will escape from the feeling of ridicule, from being no-good, an egoist, dilettante, and not serious. In the Priority of Superiority, the child feels he has worth, but is simply undiscovered. The Pleaser feels that he is worthless, "really worthless," something which becomes the secret of his life.

I recall a situation when a good friend of mine was making a surprise party for another friend. He brought me a photo album of his childhood, and we paged through it together. Between the pages of the album, filled with the ancient photos that hadn't been opened for years, was his 4th grade school certificate. In bold letters the teacher had written that she wouldn't give our friend a grade, because he didn't understand, couldn't learn, his presence in class was difficult for him and he hindered the rest of the class. My friend, who had established a flourishing public relations firm and was considered very successful, reacted traumatically to the discovery of the certificate.

I had no connection to his childhood since I knew him only as a highly esteemed and successful person. However, half a minute of confrontation with what was written in the certificate – and everything turned upside down. Our meeting ended with his anger and curses at the "cow" that had destroyed his life. Fearing that I would take note of the comment, he flooded me with explanations about what really happened in 4th grade, and then tore the certificate to pieces. My first reaction was that grade 4 did not foretell the future. His collapse when he realized that I now knew that his whole life was a lie, and in fact, what the teacher had written about him was still true – was a complete surprise for me.

The difficulty understanding the formation of the Impasse is linked to the early age at which it takes shape. For that reason I mention the topics as described above in connection with the universe and with our place in it, and particularly the nature of information absorbed by the brain which is empowered by basic imprinting,

How does laziness come about? Is it a product of a lack of energy and tiredness, boredom with a repeated performance, or forgetfulness of the goal, so that all he does becomes a meaningless *sisyphistic* task? Or does the lack of satisfaction from previous attempts at work wind up re-classifying all effort as "unpleasant?" It is a fact that small children are often reluctant to complete a task when it becomes compulsory, and since the child's behavior is observed and criticized by an adult, the negative feedback becomes a part of the imprinting.

The feeling of being frivolous, evasive, not respected, always seeking shortcuts becomes a traumatic, basic experience. As with other negative experiences, as the child grows up he learns to avoid it, to bypass it. He learns to get positive feedback, love and admiration by other means. The Pleaser will attempt to be loved and wanted all his life. Before describing the Priority in detail, I shall preface it with a few lines on love and, actually on the attempt to achieve it.

Love is an abstract concept, unfocused, hard to prove, but known to everyone. We use the concept of love daily, and are sure that it links all people, being a code that we all share. Over the years I have heard the concept of love thousands of times – as loved, not loved, not truly loved, not in love yet, or unloved, and many other versions. I pondered whether there is really is a common concept for love or does each person have his own version. There seems to be an agreement on at least one basic experience that characterizes love – admiration or at least excitement.

It's impossible to be in love without being enchanted by the other. By being enchanted there is identification with cosmic specialness. Ernest Becker's term cosmic specialness can also refer to a man who loves his dog. He is excited by it, sees something special in it.

For all its complexity, I think the major substance of the concept of love is enchantment or admiration (obviously, conditional on the person's basic ability to admire). We will return to the Impasse of our individual, the Pleaser. Since he didn't get admiration but only attention for his misdeeds or for what he didn't do, being admired will become a basic need, and become the foundation of his life strategy. It will be, the number one Priority in his relationships with the other people.

The first association with the concept, Pleaser, is an impression of a nice person, perhaps submissive, a sycophant, one who puts the other before his own needs. I have called him "nice," based on the simple test: If we invite his friends and acquaintances and ask them to describe him in one word, they will say: Nice, charming, and pleasant, or give him a nickname. He is never called David, but Davy, never Bill, but Billy. Each one has a certain trait, sometimes even a look about him, which everyone recognizes. The Pleaser will be earmarked a charmer, the nice-guy who helps everyone, knows the whole world, makes short cuts. He is sensitive to suffering, a good soul, full of charm and isn't seen a threat. He loves the joys of life and shares them generously with his companions.

Obviously the description doesn't include credible, serious, deep, etc. It doesn't mean that all these people are not blessed with these qualities; but they will never be seen as his basic nature.

The Existential Condition and Life's Strategy – The Priority

The significance of the Priority concept is fictitious, because there is no real need for any condition of our existence. We simply exist. However, to understand our place in the world we learn to play a certain role, and the more involved we become with others, the more it becomes our existential condition among them. Naturally, this condition exists only in our own eyes. In others – we simply exist. Professor Dreikurs called this condition, "only if," meaning that I have a place only if I love, I am efficient, I am silent, etc.

It is surprising that our interpretation of the events of our lives does not verify new learning about the existential condition which becomes increasingly more sophisticated with time, and self determined. The first imprinting, being – the first explanations in the brain's center of self-management, catalogues for us "the nice" and "not nice." It establishes our place in the world and continues to accompany us throughout our lives.

If so, the Pleaser is conditioned more than others by the need to be acknowledged, to "feeling felt." The ability to get attention becomes his life's focus – in conversation, in doing things, in bringing people together through his many gifts. No person is too "small" in his eyes; everyone is put in his address book and gets noticed. Being in his presence always gives the crowd a warm feeling. One day, even if your acquaintance is superficial, you will need him, maybe not him personally, not for his advice *per se,* but for his connections and the vast knowledge he has about who, what, where and when. Bringing people together is his skill, and he becomes a natural networker.

This trait in itself testifies to his continuous stream of energy, his ability to have a finger in every pie, and his fascination with people in general. Therefore, over compensation of the basic inferiority of "unworthiness" becomes the first Priority in all his connections with people. The need to get feedback, to be known, to provide a certain service so that others need him, becomes an obligatory condition of every bonding.

The prominence, the rowdiness, the ability to turn every informal conversation into subjects that he is familiar with, and do so with great charm is his special talent. What are the topics at which he shines best? He is always immersed in the realm of his experience. If the topic is about a book, it won't be a book review, it will always be: What happened to me, what I was reminded of when I read it, or I know the author or the subject because "in 1968, I was…" I, I, I…

His dimension of experience is the same with everyone – making an immediate bond. With his combination of humor and self-criticism he is fascinating. He will always answer with an anecdote; when an important name is mentioned, he knows him, of course. The story is always interesting very entertaining, personal, and upgrades him not because of who he is, but always because of who he knows.

It can be understood that discretion or accuracy about details or precise quotations don't concern him, nevertheless people continue to tell him because he is nice and impresses us.

Everywhere he goes, he enjoys attention, and presents himself with elevated importance, like: "Hey Charlie, I read that you were appointed general director. We haven't met for years but I want to congratulate you. By the way, I'm the director of…, did you know? He cherishes all kinds of accoutrements, cigars, a pipe, all sorts of gadgets, and conveys style and confidence. There is always a sweet shop nearby, a good restaurant at a short distance, where he knows the manager and all the waiters and can order a table at the last minute. A yacht, trips, holidays with the top ten percent (even if he isn't one of them). At the same time, he is equally at home eating hummus and pita with the janitor or getting a job for the secretary's daughter.

He has a finger in every pie. Every deed makes him happy. Formal meetings with him soon turn informal and casual. Every contact becomes part of "our gang," and he readily discusses one's health (knows all the doctors), gossip and interesting tales about the million people he knows. His "day's work" always includes people from all walks of life. He is fully awake, living for the moment.

It's important to emphasize that for the Pleaser, every man, old or young, is important, gets attention, and never feels threatened or inferior. If you are "higher" in rank, he will fill you with joy, form an informal relationship with you, and offer all kinds of help. If you are "below" him, he will enthuse over you without conveying the feeling of rank, and will give an immediate offer of help. The promises are not always kept but his great charm lets people forgive him – for the hundredth time, and continue to love him.

His vitality is always anchored to the present. This man gives the rest of us a feeling that what is taking place at the moment is the most important. The chat with you, the plan we are proposing, the empathy between us, this is the principle. Even if you aren't like this, you are involved momentarily.

Attitude toward Time

The present is the living space of the Pleaser. Everything is done on the spot, and there is a mass of business to do every moment. Long-term projects don't interest him. The present and the deliberations around him also signify his natural activities. He has a problem with frustration, and he'll find a thousand ways for an immediate solution even if it means making errors and being unethical in one way or another, but he won't reject anything. When long-term projects are discussed, he will always recruit others successfully.

Therapy

The Pleaser is an easy subject to treat. He is inquisitive and knows in advance that he can charm the therapist. He will make an informal bond, call the therapist by his first name may be even a nickname, will talk at great length about himself, while expectations from the therapy will be attention and immediate advice. He has trouble in being dependable, and he will treat the therapist as though it is "on line" advice is expected for every object and subject.

What will send him to treatment?

1. Couples – the ability and need to be in contact with many people, conflict with the relationship with the male/female partner. The female partner will generally be introverted, quiet, takes no part in the carnival, but also is no longer charmed by her partner.

2. Decisions – He has difficulty making serious decisions. Every situation requiring a decision is analyzed to the last detail – is it worth it, not worth it? He consults many people who only confuse him. On many subjects he doesn't feel qualified to decide and prefers an external opinion. Our happy man who loves living is extremely anxious about everything.

3. Health is an important issue and he cannot cope with being ill. He gets 2nd and 3rd opinions, his doctors are always there for him as he is for them. He has anxiety that may appear as panic attacks. He will usually contact his therapist (more than once) requesting company and instant

availability. Contact with the therapist becomes a source of reassurance.

Summary

We have to continuously remind ourselves that every one of the "types" is an active person who contributes in creating his own way.

The Pleaser is a sought after friend in any group. He communicates a lust for life, for pleasures, for "sins" that are affordable for everybody. He doesn't present a high standard, he helps and never tires of the need to charm. His basic characteristic is helping people, and people will praise him for this all his life.

Consulting the tables at the end of the book will show us that most of the outstanding traits as well as the vital energies that are annotated are expressed mainly in the world and away from home. In the family circle – the energy ebbs, the lack of a need to impress anybody occasionally allows his feelings of isolation, sadness and reflection replace it. The home is the place for resting and recharging the batteries that will be used fully in his contacts away from home.

THE CONTROLLER

Hillel used to say: *If I am not for myself who will be for me? If I am for myself only, what am I? And if not now, when?* (Sayings of the Fathers)

The immediate association made with Control is control over others. However, in discussing the associated Priority, the intention is to self-control, a control over doing something, a continual attempt to control the problems that surround us. Even not being controlled is controlling. It can also be claimed that the Controller isn't interested in controlling others, because doing so would involves them, and the truth is that our Controller is too involved to be bothered with others.

The significance of his life, in this case, is not characterized by the recognition of other people or to make his mark in history, rather it is in doing the thing itself. Even the greatest inventors in every sphere, were not involved with redeeming the whole world but each tried to solve a problem that fascinated them personally.

We will try to understand how the development of the life strategy that is principally one involving doing, problem solving and perpetual projects, which becomes achievable through hard work.

Traumatic Basic Experience – Impasse

We will once more recall that basic traumatic experiences belong to the area of negative learning. As stated in the introduction, the infant's brain is imprinted with those experiences that are "unpleasant" for him. This is an individual interpretation, and since the negative learning is primary imprinting – they will become a taboo, that says: "I will not allow myself to experience this." I'll try to describe the family in which this child was raised, and explain how his experiences are perceived by him.

The basic experience that he observes is a kind of incompetence of his parents, or of one of them, in solving life's problems. He regards the family as weak. He doesn't feel "admiration" for his parents' capabilities, and in his young mind a virtual exchange of roles already takes place. He observes the adult world around him, examines their weakness, and is frustrated by their inability to solve problems that in his eyes are definitely solvable. He is tremendously inquisitive about the world, almost everything is interesting and meaningful and worth examining down to the last detail.

It often seems that school doesn't interest him, and that he is a bad pupil. Nevertheless, many other subjects interest him. He has trouble fitting into a framework; he always needs independence, freedom to act, to pursue his own agenda. If the framework fits, that's good, if it doesn't – then leave it. This situation sometimes renders him helpless within the framework, and he can seem passive and lacking any ambition but underneath, his penetrating mind is forming ideas.

Many Controllers have difficult childhood memories of feeling incompatible with their surroundings. But these are not indifferent children: they are serious or rebellious and do not reveal their hearts desire to everyone. They hope for a better future. Disinterest, reconciliation with the prevailing wretched situation, and submission "de facto" and "de jure" is a profound challenge for them. Helplessness becomes an impossible situation.

When saying impossible we should remember, of course, that this must be understood in the context of seeking meaning. There are those who look for it in "being more" and to correct the world, there are others who love their fellow man, but in this case our hero is not interested in either alternative. When he is helpless he isn't significant, actually he feels non-existent. Some children choose not to compete and say "I can't." But here as elsewhere, each child creates his own agenda.

A friend told me about his impoverished childhood, about his parents who were really intelligent but worked in menial jobs. They, therefore, bought second-hand clothes, education was not specially valued at home, and the prevailing feeling of despair that he recalled was: "There is nothing we can do, life is tough."

His first childhood memory was as a three-year-old. They had put him to bed, but there was a commotion in the house and he asked his mother what was happening, why are people coming and going. His mother answered him gruffly that grandma (who lived with them) was dying. He was curious and asked: "What does it mean to die?" His mother answered, "to die is to stop breathing," and left the room. After his mother went out he tried "to die." He covered his head with the blanket and stopped breathing. He tried hard to stop, but did not succeed. He thought – "mother doesn't know, you don't die like that."

Other children in a similar situation will obviously react differently. Some children love their grandmas and will be saddened and cry over her death. Others will be jealous of the attention given to the event, and they will start to cry every time the event is mentioned by the adults. However our child is not particularly sad and he is uninterested in the attention of the relatives. Out of all this drama he chooses to busy himself with one thing – what does it mean to die, and can he reproduce it. He immediately tries, makes an effort, and because he doesn't die, he concludes that his mother is misinformed about death.

Such a revealing memory is typical for this kind of child and indicates three things:

1. Curiosity and the need to know.

2. Doing and practicing. Is he capable of doing everything? He is, of course, oblivious to his limitations.

3. Obliterate the reliance on the authoritative group, and the feeling that the truth is only what he can prove.

This memory lacks emotion, empathy or a fear of death.

The Existential Condition and Life's Strategy – The Priority

Use of the concept "existential condition" emphasizes the feeling that in order to feel existence and have the right to exist the person needs to act. Passivity or acquiescence is never a possibility at all; "I do therefore I am." Since a feeling of powerlessness is an intolerable situation, doing and problem solving will become life's strategy.

The stimulus for action is immediate, different, of course from "I think, therefore I am." In immediate action, which is not necessarily always needed, his life, his very existence, is achieved. Powerlessness is his basic inferiority – control is his over-compensation. The impulse is even identified in the sayings of the sages *"Beware of the children of the poor because the Law will come from them."*

The Controller doesn't expect "to be felt" – but recognized through his deeds, not the attention to his deeds, but through the satisfaction and in the doing itself. This type of person is praised for the most part, although this isn't the object of his deeds.

Most typologists, ancient and modern, don't describe the type who acts. In general, they describe traits. The Passover *Hagaddah* identifies the wise, evil, naïve, and the one who doesn't ask. The types described by Theophrastus (Aristotle's student and successor in the fourth century B.C.), include the alarmist, poser, flatterer, eccentric etc. All of these types are based on ethical and moral grounds and subdivided according to the good and the bad, but how they each behave – we don't see.

The Controller is a new category, an active person. He is described as efficient and a problem solver. He concentrates on the job itself and aims to act correctly.

From this we understand that our man of action has to be energetic and "ready to fight." In order to act correctly he needs information, studies all his life, and to some extent, enlightens his contemporaries. Our Sages have said: *"The timid person cannot learn,"* and therefore he isn't timid. He is sometimes impulsive, sometimes changing his ways and adopting a new idea that excites him. He will give time and energy to what interests him, even if there are no immediate advantages. The urge to learn gets the upper hand. You can always rely on him. He is dependable, and in order to find a solution he is willing to yield his principles.

In his childhood he encountered powerlessness, so he does his best to understand the system and learns how to mingle successfully – even if as a child the system was closed to him. We have trouble in deciding whether his insatiable ambition stems from the wish to excel and rise above others or to excel in order to do something perfectly.

If this is the case, where is he located in this world? Since his attitudes to his fellow man, or their reactions, don't interest him, there is a variety of responses to and from him. He is busy doing, and even if doing includes people, they are not his aim. The others interest him only if he can learn from them. Even his encounters with the unimportant things, from the moment he can learn something useful from them, they will become very important for him.

An example: A well known doctor was on his way to a scientific conference but was delayed because his wife's car broke down. The mechanic said that the repair would take a week. The doctor, who didn't want to leave his wife without a car for a week, ran and bought a car manual, and worked all night to replace the damaged part. The two facts – that he repaired it himself and that he had canceled the dependency on the garage were most important in his opinion, even more than the lecture he had planned to give. When he told the story he said that the thought that something that seemed simple to him should take a week annoyed him immensely. His wife was angry and told him that he didn't have to know everything in the world. She was fed up with the perpetual stimulation that he lived with. Problem solving is his way of life, and quite naturally people are drawn to him and his energy.

There will always be disappointment in your relationship when you find out that your partner really isn't interested in you, but only in the subject matter at hand. He is not even interested in himself, and does not value himself too highly. He is the eternal student, active and efficient, finishes everything he starts, contributes by virtue of his physical or intellectual effort, and finds difficulty understanding the dependency that people have on one another. He is self dependant. He can be a family man, generous, even Spartan with himself, on condition that he will be free to do his thing in the world. Some highly successful people in this world are Controllers, and as we said previously, some of the great inventors were not preoccupied with altruism or heroism but simply wanted to solve a problem.

Attitude toward Time

The Controller can be misleading in his relationship to time. On the one hand this is a very efficient man who chastises his colleagues in committee meetings and wants to reach decisions, to be efficient and not waste time. He has no time for fools or for long orations that ramble on before making the point. On the other hand, since he is his own master and needs to be busy all the time, his attention can wander off on a minor unrelated task or a new electronic gadget, and wastes hours in the process. For him it is a learning opportunity that isn't just interesting, it is important. He too, like the Pleaser, is focused in the present and has no future plans. He exploits the present fully. The past holds no interest, the future is turbulent, the focus and action is here and now.

Therapy

From the moment that the Controller discovers the world of therapy he is stimulated. The therapist must be knowledgeable and the procedure must be interesting. Since he loves to learn, he will usually be absorbed by the procedure, like a diligent student.

What attracts him to therapy? Two possibilities:

1. Those around him who complain about his egoism, his inability to devote enough time to the family, and his wasting time on his frivolities.

2. Curiosity. The Controller is an ideal subject for therapy for the right therapist. He doesn't look for attention, he wants to help himself by his own means, if they can teach him how.

Summary

Who manages best with the Controller? Another Controller. These two individuals are stimulated together on specific subjects, they don't expect anything from each other, over and above the common interest. They are not disappointed!

The Controller is a fusion of activity and enthusiasm. The contribution of these people to the world's progress is enormous, their lives point to contribution and passion. They have brought the world to where it is today.

THE AVOIDER

Rabban Shimon ben Gamliel says: *"All my life I was raised amongst the wise, and I never found anything better for a man than silence..."* (Ethics of the Fathers)

When a person's basic life strategy regarding others is "avoidance," we need ask ourselves how activity and avoidance coexist. There is an inherent contradiction in the definition of activity as inactivity.

Several decades ago the term Passive–aggressive appeared, and it filled a gap in the therapist's understanding. For the first time someone had defined non-behavior as behavior. For the first time it was stated plainly that it was possible to hurt people not just by harshness, outbreaks of anger and insults - but also by silence in situations where one should speak out or communicate. The "silent ones" can no longer hide behind phrases such as: "I didn't say a word or do anything" without admitting that such behavior can be interpreted exactly as aggression. We are social beings, communicating with one another, and developing expectations of each other and even trying to justify them is inherent to our nature. Passive-aggression is a statement; it is a behavior and a form of communication. Thus, when we describe a strategy or Priority as "avoidance," we are describing a behavior.

Traumatic Basic Experiences – Impasse

What then is the system of basic traumatic experiences that a person characterizes as paralyzing in childhood?

One possibility is that for certain reasons the child senses his family, or parents are contemptuous or an unreliable authority. The child is basically ashamed and bewildered about who he is and where he fits in. In the child's view there is a wide gap between who he is and who he wants to be, and between him and his home and family. The pride and sense of belonging that the child should feel for his parents are distorted into feelings of inferiority and shame.

Another possibility is connected to the way the child views himself. Even in the highest achieving family there is likely to be a child who has difficulties, and who completely relies on his parents. Family events such as a brother or a sister's birth, can act occasionally as landmarks of a change in a young child. Often parents recount that up till three or four years of age, the child was wonderful and advanced, and then retreats into himself, plays less and has no friends.

There is no single cause that brings about change. In the case of the Avoider child, there is a mixture of negative experiences whose basic message is: "The world hasn't given me the place I deserve." There is a gap between his elevated perception of his ability versus his inconspicuous presence in reality.

The Avoider gives up early in his uphill battle toward existential survival, and his life task redounds to passively observing the world. He observes everything, is very aware and critical of the other's weaknesses, but refuses to join in unless he is specially "invited" out of respect. His power is internal; his wisdom comes from observation and challenge rather than practical life experience. A vicious circle can result- the more the child retreats, the greater the pressure put on him, and the more he responds to the pressure by withdrawal and clamming up. He grows up by himself.

When discussing the Controller we also describe a child who faces his family in a helpless situation. But in that scenario, a basically very capable child becomes highly competent versus an inept family. Problem solving actually becomes his great power, and he will distance himself as far as possible from helplessness and inability. His major guide lines are curiosity and determination to learn about the world. By contrast, the Avoider child, who feels battered and weak, compensates for his inferiority feelings by a super-pride, as if to say "I don't need anybody." From his perspective, being in need is akin to being insulted. Both children grew up in similar family environments but relate to events differently.

The Avoider sees the world as an "enemy camp," and he doesn't believe that anyone really cares about him. Feelings of weakness, inferiority, shame and insult well up inside him and color his experiences profoundly. We can always ask why the center for self-management in his mind had to interpret the signals in this particular way. Why not in the opposite way? Have these children really failed so miserably? Has the lack of success, or just the negative experiences in his environment, lead him to being an introvert, forced to distance himself? At the outset we have said that it is not these life events but rather his personal interpretation of them, and only this that gives the experience its significance.

The Impasse represents a dependency on the other, and shame that is felt over the very necessity for this need. There is also a feeling of inferiority related to those who insulted him but it's not clear why. Put simply he builds this life strategy around the Impasse on which it is based.

Another important issue is the capacity for attachment. Expressions of endearment, need or dependency – are very difficult, and only uttered in exceptional circumstances. "Closeness from afar" is the Avoiders life style. He is constrained in close relationships, reluctant to express a need, and finds it difficult to place confidence in authority or unconditional confidence in anybody.

The Existential Condition and Life's Strategy –The Priority

Keeping a safe distance becomes an existential condition – "they shouldn't pry into my business, they shouldn't know everything about me." Avoiders are not people-oriented and this leads to an inability to connect their needs to their surroundings.

What exactly are the dynamics of the Avoider? Deep down he doesn't "feel felt." Throughout his life he has encountered questions; "Why didn't you tell me? Why is it a secret?" and he has a problem answering. Generally he avoids answering the obvious; "but there was no need to tell." The simple needs that the majority of people have – to share experiences, to get attention, to get feedback, are very limited in the Avoider's case.

The Priority, or the social strategy that our Avoider builds, relies on and is empowered by him alone. Therefore, his behavioral traits will usually be expressed with solidity, discretion and will be much targeted. His non-reliance on others is basically artificial and a cover up; no one in this world lives solely by himself. The Avoider will usually create a framework for himself that relies on those who are different -- active types, doers, problem solvers. Problem solving generally includes other people, however the inability to ask for help leaves the Avoider to himself with his feelings of failure.

The strength of the Avoider is expressed by self control and the lack of response to those around him. At the beginning of the chapter we stated that the Avoider resembles the Passive-aggressive – because non-interference in a situation where you are expected to interfere can be understood as aggression or at least can cause disappointment. The Avoider trains his surrounding not to expect anything from him. A direct communication is usually not answered, because it is interpreted as pressure. More than any other Priority, the Avoider is a slave to his temperament, which forms for him a barrier to the world. He usually does his work well, considering that work is his self-expression.

As in every Priority, here, there is also an important role for intelligence, biography, inborn talents and developing skills. We should remember that any two Avoiders will not immediately appear to belong to the same category.

It's possible that a person in a position of leadership, who all his life is surrounded by people, doesn't basically enjoy their presence and always aspires to be alone. I once had a young male client who told me about his problems of communicating with a girl, despite his attractive appearance, interesting profession, and his desire to start a family. He said that even with the most alluring woman on the most romantic evening, he felt himself to be at cross purposes with his mind longing to be home, to be alone. In order for a person to feel like this, he has to neutralize the important factor of motivation – the feeling of missing out.

Fear of missing out for many people creates the motivation to move, to bond, to act and experience. This fear can, in its extreme form, drive people to bounce from one thing to another all their lives. They will never feel satisfied, so that when in one place, and doing one thing, they long to be somewhere else.

The Avoider can resist the temptations of life, retire to his corner, occupy himself with unimportant details and never feel that he has missed out. His responses to the challenges of the world, to life's seductions, to strong motivations are the essential avoidances. There is a certain feeling of heroism, of voluntary relinquishment, however, there is also contempt for the general rat race and all those around him. The many years of restraint creates a heavy inner pressure that becomes a barrier allowing him to avoid others, both givers and receivers. This inevitably leads to certain forms of depression.

The Avoider eschews any expression of joy in life or enthusiasm. He regards enthusiasm as a loss of self control that can bring ridicule. Many find that his lack of enthusiasm dampens the spirit of others; an observation that the Avoider rejects. His difficulty in accepting this observation stems from the gap between his self-image and how others see him. He sees himself as sensitive, excitable, capable of dedication. In reality, he is not open to criticism and regards himself as "not guilty," insisting that he belongs to the category of lovers of humanity, but not of people. He is aware of his effect on others, but his self-awareness is slow to emerge.

Attitude toward Time

The Avoider is the classic observer, a constant spectator, and he analyses the world for himself. Therefore, the past interests him the most. He is a natural historian, remembers details, and connects disparate things. All his senses are directed to the past, to lofty ideas, to the abstract, on condition that they are not occurring at the moment. Because of his continual observation from afar, his experience dimensions are limited. The present is less important. The Avoider's life is a kind of continuum between the past and distant future. His is a contemplative approach, and not necessarily a practical one. Since the present is not important to him, he tends to chronically defer his tasks. Compared to the Controller who never delays anything, the Avoider is a born procrastinator. He has a very slow reaction time. He conducts a certain power struggle, to the tune of "don't make me answer," and even when he does, the answer is minimal not open to further discussion. He doesn't offer information, and doesn't get recruited to solve the problem of the moment.

To the same extent, the long response time can be interpreted as taking time to think before answering, but the delay can also be the Avoider's response to life's pressures; viz., "I don't bow to pressure, I'll do everything in my own time." If the pressure mounts up or relationships go sour, he thinks "So what! Someone else will be recruited to do it." Should the Avoider have no recourse but to deal with the problem, he will do so in a long, drawn out process.

Therapy

The Avoider is a tough client to treat. He will usually come to therapy due to pressure from his partner, his workplace, or some life crisis. He doesn't open up easily and doesn't believe that therapy can help. He doesn't think that he is transparent or truly decipherable.

If he becomes convinced that he is genuinely understood, is "felt," therapy could mark a turning point. The major advantage of therapy could be inherent in the connection itself. This connection by definition is a "relationship from afar" and from a safe place. What could help is what we in therapy call "modeling," with the therapeutic connection itself being a model for communication.

If he agrees to join a workshop or a study group, this could be an important change. Therapy for the Avoider is primarily socialization, and strengthening his sense of "feeling felt." This is possible only because he understands he is free to stop therapy at any time; in other words he remains in control.

Summary

I too, in describing the Avoider, got infected with "avoidance." I take great pains not to commit myself to a particular definition.

A woman married to an Avoider once told me that after years of attempting to activate him unsuccessfully, she too became an Avoider. Her friends complained that in the past every offer such as "let's go to the cinema" was answered immediately, while today her response is no better than "we will see …"

It's important to note that as he gets older, the Avoider becomes more remote. This is largely due to the fact that society has left him alone and given up any efforts to activate him.

There is a certain mystery about the Avoider type. From one viewpoint he is a dedicated worker, he has a certain inner flame, is focused, but nevertheless doesn't need us, doesn't seek respect or recognition. From many he will get respect and avoidance from others. However, he will always listen to those who need him and will help on condition that he is not expected to change direction.

SOCIAL ECOLOGY: THE FOUR TYPES

Knowing that our brain frequently classifies the "nice" and "not nice," so too the four types that I have described will catch the attention of the discriminating reader for good or for ill: who appeals to us, who is maddening, who we want to avoid, etc. Therefore it is important to remember that as in nature, in human society the emphasis is on ecology. There is logic in variation and balance.

In different places and different situations we are requested to behave in a host of ways. A job interview is not a stand-up comedy performance. In negotiations – for example, whether commercial or political, a balance among many people and strategies is needed: the meticulous, the unassuming, the joker who breaks the ice, the efficient, the summarizer and the one who brings everything to a conclusion.

The Sages have said: *"The shy man cannot learn nor the impatient man teach."* Each of the types described is not made from a single mold. Each of us has a virtual tool box from which to choose the behaviors to exercise, when the right time comes. Clearly, if the tool box expands through learning and experience, we possess more possibilities to match our behavior to a wider range of vital situations and challenges.

The Priorities as defined here are strategies of life. The development of personality correlates to the expansion of our strategic tool box, giving us the ability to adapt ourselves to different life situations and be capable of creating our own unique response to new and challenging events.

The President of Israel, Shimon Peres excelled in describing the distinctive values of different cultures. In a radio interview he was asked what the French left behind in their last campaign in North Africa? Peres replied: "Sophistication" and the British in the Middle East? to which Peres replied, "Administration." And in Gaza, what did Israel leave? "Democracy" was his answer. Even if these values didn't become local cultural pillars they left a meaningful, iconic impression.

Social ecology addresses the combination of the various abilities of the individuals to come together, interact, disagree, and cooperate to create the overarching social fabric of the group, the culture, the nation. No matter the group or culture, the four Priorities seem to be universal in all humans, and thereby help us understand the dominant behavioral strategy of the individual and its underlying motivation.

CASE STUDY - DANI AND YAFFA

Dani and Yaffa met when they were in their early twenties, and married soon after. Three years later they sought counseling. They sat opposite me -- two nice young people, healthy, holding hands, graciously assisting one another, and using terms of endearment.

In their words they came because they were both very irritable. In the three years they had experienced many changes, traveled abroad to study, came back and changed jobs. They argued a lot about minor things, and there wasn't an equal distribution of tasks.

Yaffa: "I do all the housework by myself and I have a fulltime job. I do all the bank accounts, and solve all the problems. I was willing to do all this because I thought I was marrying an artist. But he is very lazy, and lately is unproductive at work. He retreats into himself, listens to music for hours on end, and has no interest in sex."

Dani: "Yaffa is irritable and angry most of the time, tense, and very demanding. I feel so pressured that I can't sleep at nights, and I have developed tics and facial grimaces. Yaffa is quarrelsome, tensed up, and wants everything done on the spot. When she returns from work and there are dishes in the sink, and I am listening to music, she explodes straight away. It's a transitional period at work, and I don't know what the next step will be. In the meantime I don't do much except teach art, and this doesn't satisfy her."

"What attracted you to each other, was it love at first sight?" I asked.

Yaffa: "I was attracted because he was from Europe; he was a promising artist and a nice person."

Dani: "I simply loved her, and still do."

Family Constellation – Dani

Dani is an only child to parents who separated when he was five. His father left for good, and was never seen again. Dani and his mother lived with the grandparents and an unmarried aunt, his mother's sister. When he was eleven his grandfather died, and Dani, his mother, grandmother and aunt left Europe for Israel.

Dani grew up surrounded by independent women, career woman who always supported themselves. Their ambitions were focused on Dani, in the hope that he would become a great artist, study at the best schools, display at exhibitions, and concentrate only on his art. His every need was immediately met, and he was never expected to contribute anything to solving problems of any kind.

Young Dani had no friends, and in his words, he didn't need any. His home and family were his company as well. Family relationships were good, despite continuous stresses and competition between the two sisters. Grandmother was the "head" of the entire band. Dani decided to study photographic art, and acquired much experience in photography, since he spent his childhood and youth photographing the personae around him, as he put it.

Dani is a good-looking, serious and humorless man, who doesn't get sympathetic responses from people. He is not emotionally involved with others or vice versa. He runs his relationships "alongside."

Childhood Memories and World View

1. I remember myself sitting in a closed crib, my diaper full of pooh, and I am playing with it. I have a feeling of sitting by myself for a very long time but no one comes. I decide to try getting out of the crib. I <u>remember</u> myself climbing, opening the rail and successfully getting to the floor.

2. I was in grandfather and grandmother's house. I was sitting on the pot and doing pooh. The door was open and I was afraid that the neighbors' daughter would come in and see me – and this happened, the girl entered through the door and asked me what I was doing there. I remember myself turning around and around, inwardly cursing her all the time, and being unable to hide. I <u>remember</u> that I was afraid that she would come in even before she did.

3. I was with my father at a summer camp in the mountains. He was the organizer of the camp. At the end of the first group he returned to town with the children in order to return in the evening with a new group. He left me alone with another group, in another house. After he left I ran away to our villa, and when I got there I found that it was locked. I climbed up and broke a window and climbed in. I <u>remember</u> me lying on the bed alone and crying.

4. I was in the schoolyard, in first grade. I was running in a game, afraid of falling on the gravel, and I fell. I hurt my knees badly and I was cut. I <u>remember</u> that I was uncertain whether to run because I knew that I would fall down.

5. I was in the snow, I trod on a big box, and it suddenly crumpled up and I fell into a big hole that was covered by the box. I started to shout, but I knew that no one could hear me. I started to wrestle in the snow to get out. I felt the ground collapsing under me. I managed to get out, but one shoe was left in the snow. I remember limping home with one shoe on.

Discussion on Dani's Memories

Dani's view of the world is clearly illustrated in all five memories. First, in all of them Dani finds himself alone, forsaken. In his world view, no other people appear to be in direct contact with him. They are present only within the general framework of the recollection, and act from afar without any connection to his expectations. The only person to appear is the neighbor's daughter, in whose presence he feels exposed, ridiculed, and becomes angry at his own helplessness. This is the only "interaction" with someone else. The closeness itself is perceived as exposure to a shameful experience. Her attempts to get closer are interpreted as insulting, prying and violating his territory. In the presence of this closeness he remembers that he felt wretched and angry.

In the other memories anger doesn't appear but is replaced by sorrow and isolation. Solitude is common in all the memories, reflecting his fear feeling that he is alone in the world and the world is full of obstacles. In nearly all the memories Dani overcomes obstacles: climb out of the closed crib, breaking a window, getting out of the hole in the snow. However, the focus of his memories is not a feeling of accomplishment that he has surmounted these obstacles but on his aloneness, sadness, abandonment and loss (of the shoe). Disregarding the achievements and the initiative, Dani feels neither satisfaction or victory. His memories say that life is a great obstacle race and he must jumps one hurdle after another, endlessly. There is no satisfaction because no sooner does he overcome one hurdle before another one is already looming. In two of the memories (sitting on the pot and falling in the schoolyard) Dani knows that danger is at hand, but he is unable to avoid it. It is interesting that in most of the memories he overcomes the danger, yet he feels fatalistic – that he can't avoid the disaster, it will happen anyway. There is a complete lack of power or control over events and people – "the world isn't under my control; I might be able to manage and overcome, but I can't control it." Despite the initiative that is seen in practice, the feeling of helplessness floods him: "I can't depend on myself, I know that I shall fall – and indeed I fell. Not only am I unable to trust the world, I am also unable to trust myself. When I run, allow myself to play, and am spontaneous – I fall."

In two memories (the closed crib and the hole in the snow) we find a description of activity which overcomes and is triumphant. In this connection we emphasize that although Dani is aware of the pitfalls in life, he also knows that he can overcome. In the first and second memories the subject of excreta was repeated. His sensory preoccupation is paramount – auto-erotic, exposure of genitalia – generates a feeling of shame.

What is shame? It is a painful experience that creates the urge to hide. Shame isn't conducive to a straight look; there is a desire to be swallowed up by the earth and even to hide from the shame itself. Dani feels exposed to the small, mocking girl (the neighbor's daughter). This will eventually become a kind of prophecy that fulfills itself when he lives with Yaffa, the inquisitive and curious. Yaffa, too, like the child in the memory, wants to know his inner feelings. While Dani, in the face of the intrusion, feels powerless and debased. He therefore guards with determination his privacy – his emotions, thoughts and his perpetual feeling of helplessness.

His life is recurrently sad, filled with feelings of isolation, abandonment, and a lack of expectations. The other people are viewed as critical or mocking, never supportive. Even when the world is supportive, Dani doesn't trust it. He relies only on himself, while every misfortune that he is delivered from predicts the one that follows.

These two excreta-connected memories can also indicate anality. Between one and three years of age the child is fixated on his ability to control his bowels. Freud characterized fixation in this period as creating an anal personality or anal character. The anal personality is characterized by stubbornness, passive resistance, thriftiness/miserliness, and rigidity.

Dani's personality development can be diagnosed through various theoretical approaches. Whether we are discussing anal fixation or a cognitive world view which is supported by the explanation of his experiences, we do gain insight about his young personality as it was being formed.

From within his protected world the rest of mankind is conceived as alien, an "enemy camp." Therefore no information, weaknesses or feelings are to be given away, since, according to his pessimistic belief, this could all be used against him. He is always focused on himself, and on no one else. We recall Viktor Frankl's dictum that our life's purpose must be focused beyond ourselves for us to be significant. No man can be the target of his own life and Dani is immersed in himself, controlling his life through precognitive feelings ("I knew that the girl would arrive"). Precognitive feelings are a form of event control; however they always predict "enemy infiltration." Dani has a dialogue only with himself, there is no give and take with the world, and there is only a life of onlooker and observer.

Development of Avoidance as a Life Strategy

Following an intrusion into the psychological world of Dani the child, we immediately discern the "other" as abandoning, unable to hear his cry of distress, unable to perceive or respond to his needs. The outcome of the intrusion is a situation of shame and degrading exposure, which is the end-product of helplessness.

In his real life, events happen in a similar order: His father leaves, the ensuing shame, the pain, the child's isolation in an adult's world, and the helplessness stemming from his inability to somehow influence the big events like separation from his father, his grandfather's death, and the migration to a new land.

The social relationships and obligations of his tightly knit family and their life together became even tighter after immigration to Israel and proved very stressful for Dani. Added to that were the stressful years of adaptation and the efforts required to find his place in a new culture. All of these led Dani to "choose" the path of least resistance as an interpersonal behavioral strategy. The lesser evil between people is to avoid as far as possible involvements, confrontations, negotiations. Avoidance is in effect avoiding exposure to mockery, and being helpless. Dani perfected his power in a professional medium that was by chance photographic art. As someone who spent his life as an observer, uninvolved, he could clearly distinguish appearances and performances, knew how to catch the finest nuances and was aware and receptive to them. In situations where he had to emerge from his role as an observer and be a player, he chose avoidance.

This behavior got stronger at home over many years. The family consisted of three women, in particular two sisters, who squabbled all the time over family dominance. According to Maslow's hierarchy Dani chose security and the satisfaction of his physical needs.

In his wife's words: "Among his professional colleagues he always gives in and retracts his opinion despite the fact that he is the specialist in the group." Such modesty is apparent modesty, an effective way to avoid exposure to ridicule, criticism, confrontation, since he reckons that he has no chance to influence others. His retreat from the give and take of discussion, and his inability to be influenced are both forms of avoidance. Ceding the argument is only seemingly so, since Dani doesn't accept the other's opinions and is satisfied with his own viewpoint and convictions.

Except for his family, we see his absolute avoidance of relationship to authority in his various reference groups, including his wife's. In relationships, Dani plays the role of the child, and he completely avoids problem solving or taking responsibility. He leaves it to others to be independent, responsible and decisive. When he wants something – like a new electronic gadget he buys it without thinking or checking his financial situation. Balancing his account is his wife's or mother's job. It doesn't bother him one bit and, not surprisingly, he doesn't understand why he's been labeled a "spoiled brat"

Since closeness threatens him, getting married posed a big challenge. He did establish a good basic relationship with his wife, but he knows only one form of close connection which is based on "mothering." Soon a bond was created resembling that between him and his mother, which also led to his everlasting comparison of them. Dani begins retreating from closeness. He shuts down, listens to music most of the time, is unenthusiastic about social events, leaves the room when Yaffa invites her friends and family, and withdraws gradually from sexual relationships with various excuses. He locks himself in the other room, and frequently masturbates as he did in his childhood and youth.

In his own world he goes deeply into his photography or his teaching at school, and he takes a pedantic manner typical of an anal personality. Every time he starts on a new project he terminates it for various reasons. His plans don't proceed from the planning to the execution stage. They are general in nature, nourished especially by his mother's ambition, as for example when he cut short his studies and took another study trip abroad, for no visible reason.

Dani at age 27 is in the process of making avoidance his life's plan, effecting everything from involvement to current problem solving. He ostensibly displays indifference, lack of enthusiasm, absence of will, desire or joyfulness, and lives with a feeling of "this is not it." While all this is taking place, Dani is in a cocoon protected all the time by his wife, mother and aunt. He still works at the school and doesn't want any changes, just to be quiet, especially hoping others won't come to him with complaints and will just leave him be.

Impasse

The pain he experienced in childhood, the feeling of helplessness, inability to perform, the fear of pressure and expectations of others from him, have left him devoid of an effective "self- organization." All of these pressures are paralyzing Dani's ability to accomplish any aim in his life.

Dani's behavior, his relations with people and withdrawal into his personal shelter, indicate one clear purpose – survival. Other people are "the enemy camp" resounding with its dangers. Dani knows that he lacks any skills to win over other people, to influence them and find his place among them. Either the place is allotted to him by privilege or his talents, or he gives up and surrenders. Negotiations concerning human relations are interpreted as a dangerous existential struggle, therefore Dani avoids them. Even ambitions are looked upon as great fantasies rather than clear aims to pursue with effort.

The difficulty he has clarifying for himself what he really wants is avoidance in action. Dani realizes this through his sense of loss and his expression, "this is not it." His work at the art school is illustrative. Even though he has been working there for only a short time, he has gained respect among his colleagues, been given the opportunity to achieve new things, and communicates easily with the students. Most of the students chose to work with him in the group class. But, Dani isn't satisfied and claims: "They don't let me do what I want to." The overall feeling that the "others" threatens his freedom and existence occurs today as it did in his childhood. In contrast, his existential aim is to remain alive, to protect his freedom within his private context, and not to let others infiltrate. He still can't see the possibility of cooperation or the feeling of giving to others and its effect on him. He still only wants to be left alive, which is – he is physically satisfied – sleeps, listens to music, masturbates, being secure and protected. He is still living with a feeling of deprivation and missing out; he still lacks feelings of significance and power.

The Marriage Trap

Dani feels trapped in his marriage. At the start he was attracted to Yaffa, because she seemed to belong to the group of women in his life, connecting her with his mother, aunt and grandmother. Yaffa got involved immediately, taking on handling the daily chores that seemed to him to be "minor" compared with his art. Yaffa became the link with the world: bringing people into their lives, going out, creating an alive feeling and principally, she doesn't expect anything of him.

As time goes by, he becomes exposed to criticism and scrutiny. Unlike the women in his family –her admiration of him declined. She pointed out all his shortcomings one by one, and demanded a change. This was a new and impossible experience for him, and he responded by clamming up and retreating. In his estimation, Yaffa was intruding into his life, doing him wrong, and didn't understand him. From his perspective, she broke the key terms of the contract on which the marriage is based – that he is the passive partner, and she is the active one.

Since he is an avoider, he didn't feel the need to make a decisions or initiate a changes, or even to confront her objections. He withdrew increasingly. They fit into the equation of "fight or flight." The trap in a relationship happens when two people experience an Impasse one for the other. The man opposite us, with whom we live, represents for us all that which we are afraid of, a lack of existence and a lack of acknowledgement of our specialness.

Expansion and Growth

To Dani, all expansion means liberation from his limitations. The emergence from his boundaries signifies communication with people and not only with himself, a bridge between his inner world and the external one. For this a knowledge of the others' existence is needed, and grasping that the other is a friend, not an enemy.

Above all, the expansion will enable admission of two basic needs; the need for closeness and the need for enjoyment. All these processes will take time, he has to overcome the basic apprehension of the world, and by replacing it with a long continuum of positive experiences. Conditional to all of this is awareness of his basic avoidance, and a stimulus of his wish to live.

Family Constellation – Yaffa

Yaffa is the oldest child with a brother six years younger. Her father was a manic-depressive who was a tough problem and source of shame for the family over the years. The family came from an Eastern European country and immigrated to Israel before Yaffa was born.

Yaffa's mother was the dominant personality in the family and she took care of all the problems. They had a large extended family and she turned her home into a center for the whole clan. She arranged huge Sabbath meals, and planned frequent family visits to uncles and aunts, who became an integral part of the household. The wider family was warm and supportive, and Yaffa, even as a young girl, was expected to be the family's problem solver and arbitrator. She took it upon herself to oversee her father's behavior, to intercept his outbursts and, with her mother's full support, tried to influence his behavior. She was a "second mother" to her younger brother, and according to him, she never let him raise his head.

Yaffa was cherished and loved, positive and invaluable, and grew up alongside her mother as two close friends. In addition she was surrounded by close friends with whom she still keeps in touch. She didn't put much effort into her studies. She works as a secretary in a large business, where they rely on her and where she is appreciated. Yaffa's relationships with people are dynamic. While capable of close relationships, she is also known to engage in squabbles, jealous remarks, competing with friends and cousins, outbursts, patching up, and, in general, much emotional involvement in all her networks of connections.

Childhood Memories and World View

1. The kindergarten teacher would bring me home from the kindergarten, and put me to sleep until mother came home from work. I <u>remember</u> waking up one day and I needed to take a pee. I got out of bed quickly, but wasn't fast enough because it started leaking out of my training pants and onto the living room floor. I was startled. I took down my pants, and used them to wipe up the urine and scrub the floor. At that moment mother came in from work and to my great surprise, instead of being angry, she only said: "How nice that you are mopping up."

2. My aunt lived nearby. I was at her house and came back home alone from the top of the street. Two children were playing with a ball. I knew that the boy would do something nasty, and as I passed by, he spat on me and I think he also hit my head. I carried on home. I <u>felt</u> humiliated.

3. On one occasion all the family was sitting in my uncle's garden. They asked me to sing. I <u>remember</u> singing and all of them looking at me with admiration. When I finished the song, a neighbor came in and said she had heard the song and was sure it came from the radio. I <u>remember</u> all of them looking at me admiringly.

4. On the first day in first grade my mother didn't come with me because she went to work. I <u>remember</u> all the children standing in a line, with their parents around them. They all looked nice and clean, and I felt ugly. I <u>felt</u> humiliated.

5. They had left me with my aunts, and we sat on the balcony. A neighbor came in, looked at me and said: "such dirty eyes, such dirty hands." My aunt defended me saying she has big,

black eyes which make a shadow, making them look dirty. I <u>felt</u> as though I was an ugly dirty monkey, especially since my aunt's children were all blond and pretty.

Discussion of Yaffa's Memories

In Yaffa's narrative of her memories, firstly, they all involve people. All the memories are personalized, with interaction at the levels of intentions and action. Yaffa is surrounded by people all the time, and the accompanying pattern to this constant interaction is comparison. In some memories, Yaffa is sure she understands the others' intentions (the children will hit her, the family will admire her), and feels confident knowing what the others think. There is also insight to be gained regarding her capacity to direct the reaction of others, and her feeling of powerlessness in the face of their intentions.

The source of Yaffa's strength is hidden here as is the source of her weakness. Yaffa feels like a loser because of her very existence – her looks, her coloring, and what she projects – ugliness, monkey, dirty, black. Her feelings of inferiority get reinforced by the continuous comparison with others: the pretty children in first grade, her fair and spotless cousins, and the comparison is always to her detriment. The comparison is always made with her peers, not based on activity or equal opportunity but from the nature of things that are independent of oneself, such as ones appearance. Yaffa feels bitterly humiliated, degraded and shame.

Since childhood memories reflect an outlook on life, based on conclusions the child reaches from certain experiences, it is easy to understand Yaffa's feelings of shame and powerlessness. They are connected to phenomena that have nothing to do with her. Recall Yaffa's sick father who she mentioned earlier when describing her family background. She brought attention to the embarrassment and shame it caused the family, and the need for all of them and especially Yaffa, to conceal his behavior and protect him. She feels ashamed of something that intrinsically doesn't depend on her.

Here is a sharp division between the factual reality – over which she has no control, and the other reality in which she can act and succeed.

We experience fatalism in the face of forces that are not understood and unpredictable. She experienced the same kind of forces in the emphasis on her ugliness and inferiority. However, in her the five memories, the inferiority and helpless feelings are countered by her feelings of strength, resourcefulness, and significance. In the first memory Yaffa wipes up the pool of urine, quickly, efficiently and conscientiously, and gets rewarded with praise and admiration. In the second one, everyone admires her when she sings in front of the entire clan. Where she is left to act alone, Yaffa effectively solves problems, with resourcefully and confidence. In situations where, from the beginning, she is given a premier role ("Yaffa will sing for us") she draws strength from her audience, and gives her best. The significance comes from the others, from their encouragement and praise, and makes Yaffa feel worthwhile.

The two group-based memories represent two elements: 1. This is the world I exist in, and 2. This is my chance to act in it. In both, the world consists of other people and groups. However in contrast to the feeling of isolation, helplessness and inferiority, Yaffa finds a way to be efficient, to satisfy, to stand out and be praised, and a path to find meaning for herself.

How are the two worlds connectable; the menacing and paralytic, and the second that evokes resourcefulness, management, even triumph? To build this bridge a behavioral strategy was constructed that led her from inferiority to superiority.

Development of Superiority as a Life Strategy

We can characterize in words the sharp transition between the two aspects of these memories as "from inferiority to superiority." The definition of Personality Priority as an existential condition requires that we understand the experience of the existence and the experience of non-existence, as the individual understands them.

Non-existence is a feeling of inferiority, nullity and helplessness. In Yaffa's recollections this sensation is well described: the feeling of inferiority linked to existence itself, her personal depressed experience in the face of beauty, health, and the power of others.

The question may be asked: Why if Yaffa displayed resourcefulness in cleaning up the urine, she didn't display it when the neighbor commented or with the children in the street? What determines the choice that overcomes the power of "me" in one direction, but doesn't operate on the same rule in another direction? The others know better as in the neighbor holding s forth, the others are stronger as in the street children memory, and the happy others – clean and beautiful compared to her. This is the usual gap.

Yaffa is gifted with resourcefulness. She doesn't confront the world but circumvents it instead. She seeks pastures less central where she can sow and reap. The surprising transition from helplessness to capability takes place according to codes that she knows well. The ambition for personal "superiority" is her response to inferiority, not competition with the others. The feeling of significance for her is to be wanted, that she is needed, that she is valued her unique qualities. And what are these qualities? The first is her ability to hold back, to suppress satisfaction, to handle insults. This ability creates a form of distance or conceit characterized by thoughts such as: "It's not important what the others think," "I have no expectations from the world," "there as no free lunches for me, they're reserved for pretty girls, blondes, spotless and vibrantly healthy."

Yaffa has work to do. Because she is not dependent on entitlements or pleasure, she has the ability of doing, and understanding the others. The world has done her a good turn in creating standards for excellence, such as "to clean well." that are independent of other people.

As far as the others are concerned, Dani belongs to the group that gets the free lunch and doesn't even flinch at this privilege; it is a given, a promised land. Yaffa's "superiority" is in essence his dependence on her, in her ability to "sort out" his life, to realize her strength, "to win" as a consequence of her independence of others and no expectations from others.

However, Yaffa's strong lifestyle, her ambition and uncompromising manner, are harnessed to find a foundation and significance within the human milieu surrounding her. The ambition to overcome inferiority is really a wish for superiority. For those like Yaffa and Dani, people are a field full of hurdles. To go forward in the field one needs to acquire good skills. Only with good skills is it possible to influence and direct the world's reaction to her. Yaffa sings, Yaffa works well, solves problems and is needed. Never the less her superiority is not a steady state in which a person rises to a higher level and rest there. Life is a perpetual meeting place with others, and every time she has to prove herself anew. Life is a constant struggle. No successful workshop will change the fact that the flock outside remains skeptical and demands proof. The perpetual necessity to be the best, to win approval - resembles a well that can't be filled.

Impasse

The compulsion for superiority is the sole escape from the feeling of inferiority, notwithstanding, superiority shouldn't be misunderstood as a need to be pretentious with other people. The feeling of non-existence can only be compensated at the other extreme; to be "more" is the only way to be equal.

Yaffa's non-existence is seen in as her anxiety not to be transparent. Transparency is not thinkable, not accepted as is – for as she is, black and ugly and bearing by association, the mark of a mental disorder, she has no place. It is forbidden to see her in her nakedness. She must immerse herself in a sea of action. Even her basic functions, like the urine that escaped is a mistake that must be corrected straightaway. She has no needs, only debits. She feels as though she is unfelt and unnecessary, except by virtue of her deeds.

Erich Fromm defined human existence as two parallel tracts – to do and to be. Yaffa has no right to exist, she has no presence without doing. When necessity is absent there is no existence, she is nothing, transparent and abandoned. This is the Impasse, the motive behind all her many deeds.

After their wedding, Yaffa and Dani went to London for his studies. Now distanced from family and her close circle where she was esteemed and significant, she entered a phase defined by both of them as a mental crisis. For days on end she didn't go out of the house, lost all her will for activity, became fearful, didn't make any contacts, and was gripped by anxiety and homesickness. London was her "enemy camp," where she has no chance of being meaningful. Yaffa was immersed in a feeling of inferiority, from which she emerged on coming back home, to her real surroundings, to her family, to her former work place. Yaffa had developed a dependency on other people's reactions – if she isn't special and admired, she doesn't feel important at all, and so she declines into apathy, sadness and depression.

The Aims of Yaffa's Activity

Observing Yaffa's activity without understanding her motive could be misleading. Yaffa is industrious, a good home person, efficient and dedicated at work, meticulous about her clothes. Her home is a meeting place for her friends and family. Yaffa is a devoted daughter, visits her parents very often and takes care of them.

All her deeds are attended by the feeling of a need to prove to herself that she is satisfactory. She needs reassurance continuously, to the extent that she is unable to do things for herself, without getting the others' approval, especially that of her parents.

For this reason, being alone means a loss of motivation for action. Putting the home in order when no one can see it is not sufficient, and it bothers her to the point of bitterness and anger. Getting ready to receive guests makes her feel happy, gives her self-respect, the feeling that she is better than the rest, and she is flattered by the compliments. Yaffa hasn't learnt to act on her own behalf. The aim of her activity isn't to fulfill her own needs but to get praised by others. The others are the motive for action, without which life would be worthless.

The Marriage Trap

At her parent's home, she was the older daughter on whom they relied, and made her feel successful, esteemed and loved. She would get feedback for her actions. The reciprocal interaction of her and her family was meaningful. Yaffa was a daughter who was needed, and she derived power from her status. She played a responsible role, especially when supporting her mother and facing her father's illness, however her strength arose from the fact that her family needed her and from the synergy of this mutual need.

Yaffa didn't feel she was being exploited. On the contrary, she knew she had the power to influence, to dominate and lead the people around her. She felt close to her mother and fully respected by her, but felt angry, contempt and shame for her father. Yaffa wished to make a different kind of marriage for herself, one in which the male would be admired, successful, stable and a status creator, as least that was what she believed.

When she met Dani he symbolized all these things for her – he would be someone to be proud of. Yaffa saw the image in Dani, but not the man behind it. The psychological link between them was always that of "child" and "parent." The "child" who avoided leadership and the "parent" that knew the ways of life. Dani's Avoidance was seen by Yaffa as stability and self-control, as strength and not weakness, as security and not fear. She hoped to draw on this strength for herself, and in doing so to overcome her personal feeling of inferiority. Dani was everything she wanted – "Ashkenazi, budding artist, and pleasant" – pleasant in the sense of no pressure, and being predictable.

She quickly discovered that her relationship with Dani was in effect another version of the relationship with her father. She manages him, rules him, and criticizes him and soon found herself in the role of a "parent," a role she didn't want to play. The big disappointment of her marriage was to find herself again in the same role that she had in her parent's home. Only now, superiority didn't satisfy her. This time the audience is her new family – Dani, his mother and aunt – and they are critical, don't recognize her superiority, and who blame her. Blame is an intolerable situation for her. She, who always succeeded, feels like a failure and loses all meaning.

The feeling of being trapped rests on three failures: her inability to influence Dani, the failure to get close to a person who avoids closeness, and fruitless activity in an area where she has no chance of success – Dani's family. Yaffa is stressed, loses interest and gets depressed. This is a trap, with no way out except to admit failure or to have a complete, down and out confrontation. Both alternatives make her feel as if she is in an existential vacuum.

Expansion and Growth

For Yaffa, the marriage will continue to be a trap as long as she won't find the strength to expand her limits and conditions for meaning. Yaffa needs to learn how to act in a way that is unconditional to receiving an award without feeling exploited. Yaffa also needs to learn another form of closeness that isn't symbiotic, the kind that has privacy and the chance of letting the other live his life. Yaffa should learn a new repertoire of relationships, where the other becomes a master unto himself without draining her of value in the process. To do so she has to set her own aims, to wander in pastures that until now seemed laced with landmines – like studies, activities and inter- personal expressions with strangers, to find her place in a society apart from her inner group.

Summary

In Dani and Yaffa's marriage we encounter a meeting between Avoidance and Superiority. These two Priorities, like the other two, are constructed in order to protect the person, as far as feasible, from the great pain experienced in their childhood, the pain of humiliation, unworthiness, isolation. Each one has found their own way to guarantee their existence, by using and developing tools available to them. For Dani it was his talents and skills, and for Yaffa – her ability to serve others. Neither of them had fully expanded their repertoire of social skills that were enmeshed in childhood.

Dani still hasn't learned to discern or acknowledge other people's existential reality that can be used for negotiation. Yaffa has still to learn to be an independent person not nurtured only by the reactions of others. A meeting of these two rather extreme positions, can only occur on condition that they can allow one another to have meaning within a framework of their preferential behaviors.

However, in this marriage, as in many others, we find the paradox of two individuals living together. Specifically Dani's behavior allows Yaffa to be the "director" of both their lives. While this role, which seemed so necessary for her, now envelopes her in estrangement – which Yaffa cannot live with. In contrast, the same responsibility that Dani places on Yaffa's shoulders, so convenient for him, in turn feeds Yaffa's increasing pressures on him – a situation in which he doesn't want to live. A popular saying goes: "People don't change, they only became more like themselves." Since the marriage Dani and Yaffa seem more intensively like themselves. Dani, as the head of the family, in acknowledging the tasks, avoids even more the responsibility and the relationship, cringingly retreating into his corner. Meanwhile, Yaffa becomes more bossy and critical, and consequently is even more afraid than usual.

Out of her fear and Dani's indifference she tries to do "more of the same," while Dani - out of his fear of being trapped without an escape, which causes him pain and humiliation, flees into himself. In doing so, he also does "more of the same." In a marriage where one partner constantly stimulates the Impasse of the other – the other has no possibility of expansion and there is no chance of dividing up the functions differently from their original ones.

Specifically because of our need for validation and our search for meaning, we choose the person who facilitates us. In order that we should continue to be meaningful, we must give more of the same. In Yaffa's case, this means more solutions, more superiority, more resourcefulness, more "parenting." For Dani, in order "to stay alive" in the face of an ambitious wife, to protect himself, means retreating into a deeper ditch of absolute avoidance, and is determined never to promise anything.

Consequently, it can frequently happen that the partner who nourishes and strengthens the other's Priority, is also the one who forces the partner to withdraw into himself, with no way out.

Regarding the subject of marriage, as in the typology of personality, different approaches are recognized that aim to present the "ideal" marriage as opposed to an "incompatible" marriage.

Rudolph Dreikurs (1973), in his book, *Marriage: The Challenge*, describes marriage as a "continuous project" in the sense of expansion and continual investment. Advice concerning a peaceful home, in all religions and cultures, is similar. We are commanded to have mutual respect, consideration, placing the partner over all others in the order of importance. The Torah says: "*Therefore a man shall leave his father and mother and unite with his wife to become one flesh*", however the Torah doesn't clarify how they should live within this union, and at the same time continue to be themselves.

CONCLUSION

In conclusion, it would be correct to say we have reached an end point, but not completion. You have probably examined yourselves and your relatives, and as much as things become clearer they become less absolute. I have reduced the Personality Priorities into a table with six columns that could be further reduced. In parallel one could double the number of columns since personality is always richer and more complex than its reduction into a table.

PP is a general blueprint of social behavior. The key concept is the Impasse, derived from the inter-personal situation that paralyses us, drains us and threatens to leaves us feeling meaningless. Prior knowledge of the paralyzing factor is, according to my method, the basis for understanding the created life strategy. I divide the life strategy into four primary strategies. Why four? Because this conforms to the traditional classification. More than four is simply expansion that is often redundant; less than four is reduction. Most typologies are blessed with the secret of reduction.

We should always remind ourselves that PP is principally a therapeutic tool. Most people refer to treatment because they have difficulties functioning between "man and his neighbor," and in order to understand

and expand their personal strategy. It is important that a person diagnoses himself with the help of a counselor or advisor.

Awareness and Change

In the book, *Change*, by Watzlawick, Weakland and Fisch (1979), the authors claim that all connections between awareness and change are completely random. I share their opinion. PP is indeed an additional tool for gathering information and awareness of man with regard to himself and the world he lives in. In the process of the treatment I developed I targeted change as the central issue of treatment and awareness is one of the most important instruments involved.

Does the recognition of our behavior and even of our personal Impasse guarantee change? Certainly not.

Do we all have to make a behavioral change or a change in our world view? Certainly not.

Awareness is a map for our self-navigation and understanding others. There is satisfaction in understanding it, in acceptance, and in identification.

Part of the essence of being is the need to know. All of us have great satisfaction when we answer a question or have the answer to a television quiz - "I know it," even if we don't win a prize. We want to know, and especially the biggest unknown, ourselves. As much as we know, and our generation is blessed with more knowledge than ever before, what is hidden is still more than what is revealed, and there are many ways to look upon mankind.

I first introduced Personality Priorities in 1971 at the University of Hawaii, Honolulu, at a seminar to which I was an invited lecturer. In the audience there were professionals, psychologists, psychiatrists, experts and social workers. The audience was a cross-section of the Hawaii population: Japanese, Chinese, Hawaiians and Americans who were diverse in skin color, facial characteristics, body structure and accents.

At the end of the lecture, and in the ensuing silence, a Japanese psychiatrist stood up, approached the microphone. I anxiously awaited the question since this was the first presentation of PP. The female psychiatrist asked: "Dr. Kfir, is it true that you are an Aquarius? I wasn't ready for such a question, but of course I knew the answer. I was indeed born an Aquarius. "I knew it!" she cried. "Thank you very much." At that awkward instant I got the confirmation that there are many typologies, each with its own key.

In this course I have pointed out the principles that seem to me as basic for an understanding a person's conduct. All human behavior is goal oriented. We spend all our lives yearning, wishing, pining, and hankering for love, recognition, closeness and spiritual uplifting. Longing is imprinted in man's soul. All rivers end up in the sea, however our sea is not yet full.

We are attached together, and need one another inescapably – so that we'll feel meaningful, so that we will somehow feel special, that we matter, and so that we will know what it means to "feel felt."

Personality Priorities

The Superior

Personality Characteristics	Childhood	Impasse
Stimulated and striving	Not "discovered" in childhood	Being meaningless
Ideals oriented	Aloneness	
Useful and effective	Does not feel belonging	
Response-able (responsible)		
Self-sufficient		
Suffers nobly		

The Pleaser

Personality Characteristics	Childhood	Impasse
Charismatic	Doesn't feel competent	Being rejected
Energetic	Doesn't persevere	
Very helpful	Wants immediate reward	
'Wheeler-dealer"	Criticized	
Pleasure seeking		
Sense of humor		
People oriented		
Everybody's friend		

Table 1

Personality & Priorities

Mode of Existence	Reaction of Others	Positive Development
Aloneness (loneliness)	Recognized as special and respected	"Joie de vivre"
Doesn't spare himself	Stimulated and inspired	
Responds to suffering	Feeling of inadequacy	
Self reliant	Disappointment at lack of response to closeness	
Unequal interpersonal relations	Try to decipher him	
Creates distance		
Closeness from a distance		

Mode of Existence	Reaction of Others	Positive Development
Avoids confrontation	Hail fellow well met	Individuation and being self-contained
Wants to be loved	Is not threatening	
Volunteers to help	Taken in by charm	
Generous	Use his connections	
Manipulative faciltator	Benefit from help	
Restless	Doubt his reliability	
Anxious		
Hypersensitive		

Personality Priorities

The Controller

Personality Characteristics	Childhood	Impasse
Effective	Aware of people's helplessness	Being helpless
Responsible	Curiosity	
Needs to know	Striving for competence	
Goal-oriented	Task-oriented	
Compulsive		
Problem solver		
Respects authority and integrated into it		

The Avoider

Personality Characteristics	Childhood	Impasse
Discreet	Controlled	Being controlled
Spartan	Passive aggressive	
Reliable	Experienced shame	
Aloneness	Possible learning disability	
Introvert		
Observer		
Self-sufficient		
Detached yet caring		

Table 2

Personality & Priorities

Mode of Existence	Reaction of Others	Positive Development
Reourceulness	Respect	To case the burden
Sense of urgency	Admiration	
Compulsive	Feelimg Unimportant	
Uninhibited	Accused of being egocentric	
Competitive	Disturbing	
Assimilates and transmits information	Anger	

Mode of Existence	Reaction of Others	Positive Development
Conservatie	Good guy	Reach out
Not spontaneous	"Enigma"	
Not stimulated (by life)	Can't activate	
Too serious	Frustration	
Suffers in silence	Boredom	
Over sensitive	Lack of interest	
Avoids passion	Avoid him	
Hypercritical	Anger	

REFERENCES

Adler, Alfred. (1907) *Organ Inferiority & its Psychical Compensation*. Kessenger.

Ansbacher, Heinz and Rowena. (1956) *The Individual Psychology of Alfred Adler*. Paperback.

Becker, Ernst. (1973) *The Denial of Death*. Burnside, Hawthorn.

Capra, Fritjof. (1975) *The Tao of Physics. An exploration of the Parallels Between Modern Physics and Eastern Mysticism*. Paperback.

Capra, Fritjof. (1988) *Uncommon Wisdom*. Simon and Schuster.

Cosolino, Louis. (2006) *The Neuroscience of Human Relationships*. Norton.

Frankl, Viktor E. (1946) *Man's Search for Meaning*. Paperback

Hilgard, E. R. and Bowen, G. H. (1966) *Theories of Learning*. Appleton.

Horney, Karen. (1998) *The Neurotic Personality of Our Time*. Paperback.

James, William. (2008) *The Varieties of Religious Experience; A Study in Human Nature*. Routledge.

Kfir, Nira. (1981) Impasse/Priority Therapy. In: Corsini, R. (Ed.) *Handbook of Innovative Psychotherapies*. Wiley.

Kfir, Nira. Personality Priorities. *Journal of Individual Psychology*. 1970.

Kfir, Nira. (2002) Understanding Suicide Terror Through Humanistic and Existential Psychology. In: Stout, Chris E. (Ed.) *The Psychology of Terrorism*, Vol.1. Praeger.

Maslow, Abraham H. (1964) *Religion, Values and Peak Experiences*. Penguin.

May, Rollo. (1958) *Existence: The New Dimension in Psychiatry and Psychology*.

Prigogine, Ilya and Strenger, Isabelle. (1984) *Order Out of Chaos: Man's New Dialogue with Nature*. Flamingo.

Siegel, Daniel J. (1999) *The Developing Mind*. Guilford.

Terner, Janet and Pew, William (1978) *The Courage to be Imperfect: The Life and Work of Rudolf Dreikurs*. Hawthorn

Watzlawick, Paul, Weakland, John & Fisch, Richard. (1974) *Change: Principles of Problem Formation*. Norton.

Printed in Great Britain
by Amazon